The Bug Stops Here

By

Stephen L. Tvedten

This book is a work of fiction. Places, events, and situations in this story are purely fictional. Any resemblance to actual persons, living or dead, is coincidental.

First published by AuthorHouse 05/03/04

ISBN: 1-4184-6286-1 (e-book)
ISBN: 1-4184-4096-5 (Paperback)
ISBN: 1-4184-4095-7 (Dust Jacket)

This book is printed on acid free paper.

How to safely and simply control most household pests without harming yourself or your family.

Written by:
Stephen L. Tvedten

Compiled from The Best Control and The Best Control II.

The Bug Stops Here!

Disclaimer

The Bug Stops Here is a booklet that has been compiled for your information and the benefit of you, your family and friends; it is for reference purposes only. It is simply a small part of the information contained in The Best Control and/or The Best Control II and due to its limited size can only cover a few of the thousands of safe and far more effective alternatives the Author has described elsewhere and it can only consider the basic type of pest, such as ants, roaches, rats and other pests that can plague our every day lives. The Bug Stops Here can not and does not consider the individual species and/or conditions, nor can it be used to accurately diagnose individual pest control problems or solutions. The Author freely admits, and continues to do so, that he is not a certified industrial hygienist or graduate physician, entomologist, toxicologist, epidemiologist, chemist, pharmacist or scientist. The amazing thing is, even being so "ignorant," the Author can see the problems with "registered" pesticide poisons. The Bug Stops Here is not intended to prescribe medical or veterinary treatments and can not replace the advice of a health care professional. If you have a medical condition - be sure to consult your physician or veterinarian for medical advice. It is important to remember that when using any alternative, or when making any application of any substance, you should always test spray/wash a small area before doing any total treatment or any large application. All of the alternatives herein have been given only as general use suggestions to replace pesticide poisons. If in doubt, always use the safest method possible, including leaving the problem or situation alone. There is virtually nothing on this earth that can not be misused or will not irritate someone. The Author makes no specific recommendations for any individual situation or person. Unattributed opinions are probably the Author's. The Author and the Publisher assume no responsibility for misadventures related to the use of products and/or procedures mentioned herein. When The Bug Stops Here was being compiled and written on his kitchen table, the Author was aware that in the process mistakes, typographical errors and the like were bound to happen. The Author freely admits this work may contain some misspellings, errors, misconceptions, unsubstantiated, prejudiced, antiquated and/or even misleading data based on the many human conditions that exist. The Bug Stops Here is intended only to begin to show what brought the Author to discard the use of volatile "registered" pesticide poisons after 35 years of pest control work and to find, discover, research, field test, invent and/or try literally thousands of alternative pest control methods that are safer, more effective and less expensive than "traditional poison controls." The Author has field tested these unregistered alternatives in groves, fields, orchards, homes, offices and in over 350 schools, inside and outside, and has virtually eliminated all the pests in all these schools and areas without ever using volatile pesticide poisons. If even 1% of the enclosed pesticide problems and statistics about "registered" pesticide poisons are true, it makes no sense to continue to use them, but the real proof of the accuracy of this manual is not in poison statistics, but in the fact that these safer methods actually have been used to control pests far better than "registered" pesticide poisons do.

INTRODUCTION

by Stephen L. Tvedten

On September 11, 2001, terrorists attacked the World Trade Center in New York City, NY and the Pentagon in Washington, DC; that forever left an indelible mark in the minds of many as to the carnage and damage that occurred in terms of lives lost and injuries sustained (immediate and long-term) to people and to the environment, especially to those people living in and around Manhattan. Initially, representatives from the U. S. Environmental Protection Agency (EPA) led the public to believe that the air was "safe" to breathe in New York City near Ground Zero and, more than four months later, reports of the damage caused to the respiratory systems of people by the contaminants are referred to as the WTC Cough. On Saturday, February 23, 2002, a front page story and headline in the New York Newsday, one of the four major dailies of New York City, stated:

"EPA WATCHDOG: DON'T LEAVE HOME WITHOUT IT - Advises Respirators Be Worn Around Ground Zero"

Approximately one month after 911, government officials, who are elected and appointed to help defend and protect us, began to (all of a sudden) be concerned about the terrorists using their "registered" pesticide poisons in a follow-up attack on the American people. Some of the measures taken were that information regarding pesticides were removed from web sites and the aerial spraying of the deadly poisons was temporarily halted.

If our government officials were so concerned about these deadly poisonous pesticides being used against us by terrorists, then why in the world are they being allowed to be used at all as "registered" by them to be used in our homes, gardens, schools, buildings and elsewhere on this planet? Read on and come to your own conclusions about the uses/misuses of "registered" pesticide poisons and the damages they can bring. Read on and discover for yourself what can be done to reduce and or totally eliminate the uses of any "registered" pesticide poisons in the environment surrounding you, your family and your friends.

A Brief History Lesson...

Volatile, synthetic pesticide poisons by their very nature and design are not natural or normally occurring materials; they are man-made poisons specifically designed to kill and to contaminate, destroy, injure and/or negatively affect life.

Organophosphates were originally designed to kill or incapacitate people; these poisons are designed to be broad spectrum killers and are not species specific and have always attacked and negatively affected nontarget species, including man and his animals. The Toxic Times, "Is School Air Making Children Sick?" noted: The U. S. Environmental Agency states that "indoor air is found to be up 70 times more polluted than outdoor air" and "because most people spend more than 90 percent of their time indoors, the quality of the indoor environment and how it affects health should be a top priority for everybody who has an impact on this environment." The American College of Allergists has said that 50% of all illnesses are either caused by or aggravated by polluted air.

As you begin this ever-evolving study of true IPM or Intelligent Pest Management™, always remember the purpose of this study is to help save the earth and you from unnecessary pollution and give you better and safer pest control. There obviously will arise traditional pest control "experts" who will critique this and all of my other work. Pierre Pachet (Professor of Psychology at Toulouse in 1872) once wrote "Louis Pasture's theory of germs is ridiculous fiction!" These same "nit pickers" will be the same people who have contaminated the entire world with their "registered" poisons. To all those "experts" I simply remind them that some other "experts" assured us that asbestos, tobacco, DDT, chlordane, PCBs, kepone, silicone breast implants, lead plumbing and leaded gasoline were all once proclaimed "safe" by government "regulators" and industry. Later they were all banned or severely restricted due to adverse health effects they continually caused including cancer, nerve damage, and birth defects...**Just another example of yesterday's "solutions" becoming today's problems.**

Examples of the How Typical Pest Control Measures Can Hurt Children

A June l998 study by Philip Landrigan, M.D., Professor of Pediatrics at Mount Sinai School of Medicine in the Environmental Health Perspectives compared two culturally and genetically similar groups of Mexicans/Indians. The amount of pesticide contact was comparable to what is typically used in the USA for crops. One-half the children who were exposed to a total of 80 pesticide crop applications twice a year. This group was drastically different than the similar control group which had virtually no pesticide exposure.

Four to five year olds that were exposed to "registered" pesticide poisons:

- **could not remember what they were told 30 minutes later,**
- **had less stamina,**
- **had decreased fine eye/hand coordination,**
- **could not draw a stick figure, they could only scribble**
- **had many disruptive behavior problems, particularly aggression.**

This study raises very important concerns about the toxic effects of pesticides on children's brains and nervous systems. Bernard Weiss of the Department of Environmental Medicine at the University of Rochester

School of Medicine and Dentistry stated that the study highlights the need for more research, "It doesn't seem a surprise that you would see an effect, knowing what we know about pesticides and the elevated vulnerability of the developing brain."

The main problem with pesticide poison contamination is that you cannot see it, or at times even smell it. You cannot always determine that you are being exposed to is a dangerous pollutant and, therefore, many people still do not believe these pesticide poisons can adversely affect their health.

Studies now are proving that poor indoor air quality (IAQ) damages our health and our possessions; it lowers our productivity at work, and it diverts major resources that are needed to diagnose and solve health and emotional problems that result from this toxic contamination.

We have totally forgotten how to protect ourselves and how to successfully wage war on our pest enemy. There are about 10 million insects; we have named about 1 million and there are only about 1000 insects that are considered to be pests. Over half of the insect pest species are now pesticide resistant.

Many other well intentioned "protective" practices of the past have resurrected themselves today as threats. Arsenic was used from the Civil War to 1910 as a major part of embalming fluids; asbestos was installed to fireproof structures; landfills were intended to improve sanitary conditions and pesticide poisons were originally supposed to "protect" us against the damaging effects of insects, rodents and weeds. TRIS (was a fire retardant in children's night wear) that exposed 60 million children to a potent cancer-causing agent in order to keep them "safe;" these chemicals and many other toxins were once marketed as "safe" and "necessary". Potential adverse health and/or environmental problems were simply not a concern at that time. All or these previous "protective" practices started out being sold as "cures"!

Today we must be concerned not to allow any more "protective cures" come back to haunt us. Just a few of the problems with volatile, pesticide poisons are as follows:

A. Volatile, pesticide poisons do not stay where they are sprayed...they volatilize (are gaseous) so they can drift all over and contaminate all surfaces, people and pets.
B. Pesticide poisons do not discriminate what they kill. Any form of life is at risk.
C. Pests can quickly become immune or resistant to dangerous synthetic pesticide poisons. People do not seem to be capable of doing this.
D. Pesticide poisons are often stored in our fatty tissues, where they can become carcinogenic, or emerge later to harm us again.

E. Virtually all pesticide poisons are neurotoxins and this includes many of the misnamed "inert" substances such as xylene and toulene which are toxic solvents for many pesticides.
F. Many pesticide poisons contain contaminates or are changed into even more deadly poisons (metabo- lites) as they age or enter our bodies.
G. Most contain unregistered and untested "inerts" that often are more dangerous or contaminate longer than the active or major or "registered" poison ingredients in a pesticide formula.
H. The Tulane-Xavier Center for Bio-environmental Research in New Orleans said that combining two substances common to *registered* pesticide poisons can produce a synergistic impact on hormones 1,000 times stronger than either poison alone - but no one routinely tests for these synergistic effects.
I. The average home today contains more chemicals than were found in a typical chemistry lab at the turn of the century!

One day (hopefully in the near future) people will be astonished we actually paid someone to contaminate our homes, schools and work areas with volatile, synthetic pesticide poisons, just as we now wonder about the mental stability of people who actually paid someone to put dangerous asbestos in older buildings.

Black's Law Dictionary defines "intoxication" as a situation where, by reason of taking intoxicants, an individual does not have the normal use of his physical or mental faculties, thus rendering him incapable of acting in the manner in which an ordinary, prudent and cautious man, in full possession of his faculties, using reasonable care, would act under like conditions. **Becoming intoxicated by chemical poisons can produce a behavior that is not very different from that of a person who is intoxicated with alcohol.**

About 6,000 new synthetic chemicals are added to our environment in just the U. S. every year! Middle-aged human bodies now contain on average 177 organochlorine chemicals. Steinman, D. and Wisner, R., Living Healthy in a Toxic World. Today we have 500 to 1000 chemicals residing in us that were not there in 1920; we have become full of toxins - intoxicated - only apparently we can't sober up! To add even more toxic, volatile poisons to this cesspool we carry is truly absurd! Especially if these volatile poisons do not even control the target pests!

Obviously, we no longer have the normal use of our faculties. It is time to get clean and sober and use some Pestisafes® and common sense!

Like Lemmings to the Sea -

The American College of Allergists has said that 50% of all illnesses are either caused by or aggravated by polluted indoor air. As you begin this ever-evolving study of true IPM or Intelligent Pest Management®, always remember the purpose of this study is to save the earth and you from unnecessary pollution.

Dow Shalt Not Destroy Thy Indoor Air Quality (with Synthetic Pesticide Poisons)

Our Indoor Air Quality (IAQ) has too long been neglected even though it is as necessary to our survival as our next breath. With each breath we take in billions upon billions of air molecules. G-d help us if our ambient air is routinely polluted/contaminated with poison(s)...for unlike smoking, which we can choose to quit, we cannot choose to stop breathing! We can and must, however, now choose to stop spraying any volatile poisons in our buildings and vehicles where we spend 90% of our time.

Volatile, synthetic pesticide poisons are the only toxic contaminants the poison industry has been deliberately adding to our environment. There will be no indoor air pollution if we stop contaminating it with poison in the guise of *protecting* ourselves and our children! On particularly smoggy days, children, elderly people and people with respiratory problems are told to stay inside to avoid health risks from air pollution...yet monitoring studies have consistently found concentrations of many air pollutants are actually higher inside than outside our vehicles, homes, schools and offices!

According to the Congressional Research Service, "...Urban and suburban (synthetic pesticide poison) applications to lawns, golf courses, roadsides, public buildings, and to homes and apartment buildings can lead to even broader human exposure than agricultural applications of these toxins. These...applications can cause immediate toxic reactions (especially) to sensitive individuals...(There is (also) concern about less visible but longer-term health effects." Even with the "concern" not much has been studied about chronic pesticide exposure indoors where people spend more than 90% of their time.

In an effort to help stop the toxic contamination of our children, in 1993, EPA distributed to school districts across the nation brochures encouraging pesticide poison use reduction and alternative pest control methods through integrated pest management. Sadly, only pesticide poison applicators are mandated and/or are being hired to create the reduction! "Foxes guarding the chicken coop." EPA, FDA and USDA agreed in 1993 to find alternatives to their "registered" poisons. In 2001 Senator Leahy noted that there had been a 40% increase in annual pesticide usage since 1993. At the time of this writing, no government "regulator" was able to even define the word "alternative" when asked by the Author.

The premier total exposure assessment methodology TEAM study was the first and the largest governmental study that attempted to determine if persons living close to chemical plants and petroleum refineries had higher exposures to toxic volatile organic compounds than persons living a few miles away. No such effect was found at any of the study sites...but it did find the real danger - the median air concentrations of the 18 targeted chemicals ranged from 2 to 20 times higher inside participants' homes than in the outside!

The simple fact is our homes and/or buildings remain sealed and/or are now highly energy efficient and these inside environments are not subject to most degradative processes that exist (outside) in the sun, rain and wind - these interior conditions allow volatile, synthetic pesticide poisons to become far more concentrated and to remain active/dangerous for far longer periods than if they were applied outside. When they are applied outside in fields often migrants are not allowed to reenter outside fields for up to 4 days! Why then do you "think" it is safe for you and your family to reenter your "fumigation chamber" in a couple of hours?

In the March/April 1992 "Archives of Human Health" issue, Hebrew University School, Jerusalem and Tel Aviv Ministry of Health, et al published a study wherein they documented illness and excretion of organophosphate metabolites four months after a household pest extermination clearly indicating it is not safe to reenter a building treated for roaches after a few hours, but that toxic exposures from labeled usage may be prolonged, continuous and involve infants and children.

A few interesting facts on pesticide poisons were reported way back in a 1993 issue of USA Today Magazine:

One billion pounds of pesticide poisons were routinely added to the environment every year (back then). If put in 100-pound sacks and laid end to end, they would have completely circled the world! NCAMP wrote in 2001 we now use 4.5 billion pounds of "registered" poison...just in the USA! We truly are on a chemical treadmill that causes far more problems than it "solves".

In the 1990s EPA estimated that one out of every 10 public drinking water wells in the U. S. contained pesticides (poisons), as well as more than 440,000 rural private wells. At a minimum, over 1,300,000 people (routinely) drank water contaminated with one or more of these dangerous poisons back then! Pesticide poison contamination has been found in thousands of lakes, rivers, and waterways throughout the nation. Agriculture is the number-one source of surface water pollution in the U. S.

The rather startling figures coming in from testing homes throughout the U. S. show approximately 75% of all our homes built before April of 1988 are routinely being found to contain (significant) air levels of the previously "registered" pesticide (poison) chlordane. A study by Dr. Richard Fenske at Rutgers University in New Jersey found at least 34% of homes built before 1982 contained air chlordane levels over the (original) evacuation limit of 5 micrograms per cubic meter of air, an *interim* evacuation level set by the Air Force and the National Academy of Sciences.

Although there is no definite data on the number of homes in the United States that have been treated with chlordane, in 1987 the National Pest Control Association estimated that 1.5 million homes per year were treated with these *registered,* volatile carcinogens for termite control. Taking the information from several studies regarding chlordane contamination being found in homes today, it could be estimated that a minimum of 100-185 million U. S. residents may be breathing significant levels of chlordane contamination in their homes daily and 10-20 million U. S. residents could be living in dangerous homes where the indoor air levels of chlordane are exceeding even the recommended *interim* evacuation level originally set by the National Academy of Sciences and the U. S. Air Force, but now greatly reduced.

Once the scale of this poison pollution problem is finally brought to the publics' attention, it should dwarf the concerns generated by indoor levels of formaldehyde and radon. In a review of the chlordane home contamination problem and its link to childhood cancers and blood disorders, Dr. David Ozonoff, of the Boston University School of Public Health stated, *"a national program for monitoring all homes treated is urgently needed to detect persistent (termiticide poison) contamination."* If this wasn't enough to be concerned about, Dr. Ozonoff s went on to say, *"It should also be noted that (previously "registered") commercial chlordane formulations (also) contain carcinogenic (unregistered) "inert ingredients" and contaminants, such as propylene oxide, hexachlorobutadiene, and carbon tetrachloride, apart from some 40 other ingredients so far undisclosed by the manufacturer, formulators and applicators of C/H (chlordane/heptachlor)."*

COMMON DANGERS FOUND IN PESTICIDE POISONS

Pesticides can enter your body through the air you breathe, the pores in your skin, the fluids and foods you ingest, the clothing and fabrics you wear, and the surfaces you touch. Many affect our liver, kidney, bladder, bowels, muscles, brain and **especially our immune, reproductive and nervous systems**. Those whose daily occupations involve pesticide exposure are certainly at a seriously increased risk.

Pesticide Poisons - If you are going to use any pesticide poison to "solve" a problem, look carefully at the label and ask for the Material Safety Data Sheet (MSDS). You should be able to figure out at least part of the components and inherent dangers in the product you are questioning. First call the manufacturer's emergency number on the MSDS. The number should be on the label and/or the MSDS sheet or call 1-800-555-1212. If in doubt about a poison, you can simply use a safe and far more effective alternative.

Food Products - *All You Can Eat, Environmental Working Group (EWG) Web Site, January 1999* Interactive web site allows users to determine what pesticides they consume on a daily basis and their potential health effects. By selecting items from a list of foods, visitors to the site can access EWG's search engine that matches foods against more than 90,000 government lab test results for pesticide food residues. Provides suggestions for minimizing pesticide residue intake. Web site: www.foodnews.org.

Cancer-causing Products - *U. S. Environmental Protection Agency (EPA) Pesticidal Chemicals Classified as Known, Probable or Possible Human Carcinogens, Web Site, 1999* Provides U. S. EPA Office of Pesticide Programs' most current list of pesticides categorized by carcinogenicity. Lists registration date, use patterns, and regulatory status. Web site: www.epa.gov/pesticides/carlist/table.htm.

You can call the National Pesticide Telecommunications Network @ 1-800-858-7378. They are open 7 days a week from 6:30 a.m. to 4:30 p.m. Pacific Standard Time for any questions that you may have about the use of pesticides.

In 1992, Dr. Kenneth Rosenman, M. D. from MSU noted less than 1% of the doctors even report occupational contamination problems and most hospitals do not have a method to track pesticide poison related incidents; even so, there were 50 cases of accidental poisonings reported in Michigan. 50% of the cases requiring hospitalization from pesticide poisonings were children under the age of 12! Remember, **Dr. Rosenman estimates less than 1% of all employers and doctors even bother to comply with the current pesticide poisoning reporting requirements.**^

WHY 99.9 PERCENT IS NOT AND SHOULD NOT BE GOOD ENOUGH - If 99.9% reduction in poison use is compared to other "things" - We would have to accept:

- one hour of unsafe drinking water every month;
- two unsafe plane landings per day at O'Hare;
- 16,000 pieces of mail lost by U. S. Postal Service every hour;
- 20,000 incorrect drug prescriptions every year;
- 500 incorrect surgical operations each week;
- 50 newborn babies dropped at birth every day;
- 22,000 checks deducted from the wrong bank accounts each hour;
- 32,000 missed heartbeats per person per year.

"Never give in, Never give in, never, never, never, never - in nothing, great or small, large or petty, never give in, except to convictions of honor and good sense." - Winston Churchill

True IPM or Intelligent Pest Management® (IPM) means fighting or controlling pest infestations in ways that are least toxic to people, pets and the environment. True IPM, when properly practiced, removes the cause rather than continually and needlessly "treating" the symptom with volatile, synthetic pesticide poison! Knowledge of the species, local breeding areas, feeding and territorial habits of the pest is essential to controlling pest populations. **In true IPM, often even the pests are not killed**.

INTELLIGENT PEST MANAGEMENT®

The Art of War - In any war, one must have a sword (an offensive weapon) and a shield (defensive protection) - when we choose to only use volatile, synthetic pesticide poisons to "control" pests, we have no shield, no protection and our only "weapon" is attacking us and not our enemy.

Early in the 1990s we knew that in our ongoing war against home and garden pests, over 70 million American households made more than 4 billion pesticide applications each and every year. At least 85% of Americans or 84.5 million households maintain a poison arsenal of at least 3-4 synthetic poisons ranging from no pest strips, pesticidal shampoos, aerosols, granules, liquids and dusts. There are over 21,000 different over-the-counter household synthetic pesticide poison products containing over 300 active ingredients and as many as 1,700 "inert" ingredients per a 1990 EPA study prepared by Research Triangle Institute. The "National Home & Garden Pesticide Use Survey" found at least 75% of all American households use insecticide poisons, and consider cockroaches and ants as their leading pest enemies.

In 1993, there were over 140,000 reported pesticide poison exposures; 93% of these involved home poison use reported nationwide to poison control centers - about 25% had (acute) pesticide poisoning symptoms (over half involved children under 6).

The poison *industry* is very aware that volatile, synthetic pesticide poisons kill beneficial insects and fungus better than they do the pests. One University that tests pesticide poisons on pest populations for the poison *industry* wrote me how they use synthetic insecticide poisons and fungicide poisons to protect their pest populations! An example of predator-prey relationships that are adversely affected by pesticide poisons is a black fly predator, the caddisfly, which is susceptible to permethrin at rates lower than those necessary to control blackfly. The phytoseiid mites have an LD_{50} 15 times lower to permethrin than the spider mites on which they prey. Obviously, many beneficial insects, e.g., bees, are also killed when one "treats" pests with volatile, synthetic pesticide poisons!

The Chinese Sage, Sun Tzu's "The Art of War" written in China 500 B.C. clearly warned: "There has never been a protracted war from which a country has benefited."

Dr. Leaky has now estimated that we are losing approximately 50,000 to 100,000 species of plants, animals and insects every year because of man's "footprint". Yet after waging an ever increasing war on insects pests, using enough "registered" poison to literally contaminate the entire world and every living organism, we have not even controlled, much less eliminated, even one pest species!

Since the 1940's advent of volatile, synthetic pesticide poisons we have waged an ever increasing protracted war against pest populations and now our air, water, food, mother's milk, blood, and adipose tissue all "normally" contain significant residues of these poisons, their metabolites, their "inerts" and contaminates! We have suffered an ever-increasing array of health effects, damages, and deaths - yet our pest "enemy" continues not only to flourish, but to increase. We have continually killed our own allies (the beneficials), poisoned our own water, air, and food and, thereby, sickened, wounded or killed ourselves and our own forces and continually ignored our enemy's natural weaknesses and engaged in warfare using only one (useless) weapon! We have totally forgotten how to protect ourselves and how to successfully wage war on our pest enemy.

In 1950 fewer than 20 species of insects showed signs of synthetic pesticide resistance. In 1960 Rachel Carson had documented 137 species were resistant to at least one pesticide poison and noted it was the early rumblings of an avalanche of synthetic pesticide resistance. By 1990 the number of documented pesticide-resistant insect and mite species was 504 and, obviously, is still increasing. In addition to over one-half of the resistant pest insects and mites, we have many other pesticide resistances developing, e.g., bacteria, fungus, weeds, etc. **Volatile pesticide poisons do not effectively control, much less even diminish the pests against which they are continually used/misused!**

In 1993, 1 in 7 Americans got cancer. We have spent many billions of dollars on cancer research (a river of gold); yet now 1 out of every 2 Americans will get cancer and in the near future, breast cancer will be the #1 killer and prostate cancer will be the #2 killer of Americans! In the 1990s, one in eight women got breast cancer.

From 1960 to the 1990s, more than 950,000 died from breast cancer - almost half of these deaths had occurred in the last 10 years! Putting this in perspective - only 617,000 Americans have died in all the wars our country has fought this century! Unless we desire the demise of our own race, we must stop releasing tons of virtually untested, unstable, synthetic pesticide poisons that are creating a synergistic contamination that no one can honestly say they can truly assess all of the human health risks for and which still does not even control our pest enemy! Some of the "inerts" can continue to contaminate for much longer than the active poison ingredients, e.g., some *inerts* have a half-life of greater than 880 years!

Yet, the U. S. annually now blasts itself with about 4.5 billion pounds of volatile, synthetic pesticide poison which, obviously, provide fewer and fewer "benefits".

By 1964, 2/3's of all U. S. insecticides were used on only 3 crops: cotton, corn, and apples per the Mrak Commission (In 1969, the U. S. Department of Health, Education, and Welfare prepared a landmark report on the environmental health consequences of pesticides - The Mrak Commission). Pimental et. al., in Environmental and economic impacts noted that despite a thousand-fold increase in the U. S. use of insecticide poisons on corn-losses to insects have an increased 400%!

Cornell University researcher, David Pimental in Silent Scourge, Audubon, Jan./Feb. 1997 estimates that of the roughly 672 million birds annually exposed to pesticides in the U. S. - 10% - (at least) 67 million - of our allies are killed annually! (Note: Back then, about 5 to 6 billion pounds of insecticides, herbicides, fungicides, rodenticides, and other biocide active ingredients were yearly added to the world's environment.)

The concepts of synthetic pesticide resistance, pest resurgence and the development of secondary pest problems have been taught (and then ignored) in introductory science classes for literally decades! Since synthetic pesticide poisons were introduced into agriculture at the end of World War II, total crop losses due to insect damage (despite a tenfold increase in insecticide poison) have almost doubled - from 7% in the 1940's, when all agriculture was essentially organic, to 13% by the end of the 1980's. In 1945 almost no insecticide poison use was used on corn and the USDA noted insect damage only averaged about 3.5%. In the 1990s, despite more than one thousandfold increase in the use of synthetic insecticide poisons on corn, losses to insects then averaged 12%! Entomological Journals are filled with pesticide resistance problems developing all over the world - obviously, synthetic pesticides quickly create resistant or immune pests. **Pestisafes® normally do not create resistant or immune pest species!**

In the 1990s approximately 5% of all farms controlled over half of the Nation's agricultural production and our smaller farmers were already going out of business by the thousands, all while economic consolidations using mergers, takeovers, and conglomerations in the food and poison industry are being magnified a hundred-fold - we now are almost totally dependent on the poison industry - and their resulting contamination for our "food".

In 1981, A. Robert Abbou'd as president of Occidental Petroleum, a giant energy corporation, spent $800 million to acquire Iowa beef processors and said "we're going to be running onto a food scarcity situation in the 1990's in the same way we have an energy shortage in the 1980's. We will continue to build in this area." Occidental Petroleum also is known for its Hooker chemical subsidiary and Love Canal controversy/contaminations.

A few multinational corporations and "banksters" now own the new "biotechnology" that is genetically altering or "modifying" all of our (hybrid) seeds, livestock embryos and/or other living organisms - shifting the ability to produce food from our farmers to the "scientists" and therefore to those that actually own them, their "science" and their chemical poisons and their patents - all at the expense of environmental safety, nutritional value, and biological diversity and therefore our future (altered) harvests - all are sacrificed on the corporate altar of expediency and profit - yet we still are being told the same old propraganda/lies that there still is nothing to "worry" about - "Hold still please...Trust in me, just in me...Shut your eyes..." - the snake, Kaa, in The Jungle Book.

We can no longer produce our own seed as farmers did since the beginning of time. Genesis 1:12: "and the earth brought forth grass, and herb yielding seed after his kind, and the tree yielding fruit, whose seed was in itself, after his kind; and G-d saw that it was good." **Today we must look to man and not G-d for our daily bread.**

The clarity of Sun Tzu's thought is still acted upon by Chinese generals of today; it is **"The supreme art of war is to subdue the enemy without fighting."** This supreme art is what I have continually developed upon in my intelligent pest management® manuals, The Best Control© and The Best Control II© and this little book. I, like Sun Tzu, believe "The skillful strategist should be able to subdue the enemy's army without engaging it, to take his cities without laying siege to them, and to overthrow his State without bloodying swords".

One of Sun Tzu's admirers was Mao Tse Tung - in Chiang Kai - Shek's army - most of the younger officers considered Sun Tzu's thoughts to be out-of-date and hardly worth study in the era of mechanized weapons. Chairman Mao Tse-Tung disagreed with his enemy and in May, 1928 wrote "on protracted war", selected works Vol. II page 156 that "The object of war is specifically to preserve oneself and destroy the enemy" (to destroy the enemy means to disarm him or "deprive him of the power to resist", and does not mean to destroy every member of his forces physically.).

This "truth" taken from the "Little Red Book", contains the essence to true IPM. To use toxic, volatile poisons that do not preserve us, but rather destroy our own people, pets, and natural allies without even diminishing, much less destroying our pest enemy, but which in truth actually preserve our pest enemy and even prosper our pest enemy is to insure the annihilation of those living things (including yourself) you are trying to protect and preserve!

All of the guiding principles of military operations grow out of this one basic principle: to strive to the utmost to preserve one's own strength and destroy that of the enemy ... to release nerve gases, hormonal disrupters, carcinogens, mutagens, etc. (poisons) into or onto one's own person, ambient air, food, or water is to insure our own eventual defeat or destruction - while preserving that of our resistant enemy, and totally ignores the basis of all successful military principles! The communist Chinese Red Army defeated General Chiang Kai-Shek using this very principle and Mao noted that "without preparedness - superiority is not real superiority and there can be no initiative either. Having grasped this point, a force which is inferior, but prepared can often defeat a superior enemy by surprise attack." I warn you our "inferior" pest enemy is already resistant to our "superior' pesticides and is already winning the war - common sense (which is not too common) and the use of true IPM as detailed in the Intelligent Pest Management® manual, The Best Control©, The Best Control II© and this little version will yet turn the tide in our favor.

The purpose of True Integrated Pest Management or Intelligent Pest Management® or Imaginative Pest Management or Innovative Pest Management (IPM) or Ecologically Based Pest Management (EBPM) is to render an area more or less permanently uninhabitable for the pest - in as environmentally safe a manner as possible...often it does not even destroy the pest. Rather than simply trying to control pests temporarily at best, using volatile, synthetic pesticide poisons which are very harmful to people, pets and the environment, IPM is dedicated to removing the causes rather than treating the symptoms. Passive IPM is simply allowing natural programs, predators and controls to remain in place. Active or true IPM can be easily understood if you can relate the pest's needs to your own needs and home.

If you came home and found every room was filled with foam or concrete (caulking) or that your home had been altered so that your heating/air conditioning were not working or were removed (temperature changes) all the locks changed and/or all windows and doors were boarded over (exclusion) and/or steel bars were installed over all windows and doors (screening) all plumbing, gas and electricity lines removed, all food supplies, clothing, furniture and beds either removed or secured in such a way you could not gain access (sanitation and habitat reduction) to your own home or even the things you need to survive you would move - if you still did not move the police would come and take you away (vacuums and/or traps). You now can understand how we will use true IPM techniques to permanently eliminate the conditions conducive to an infestation and, thus, the pest. **All of us are capable of waging war on pests, directly or indirectly, especially using Pestisafes® and common sense.**

What we must first understand is our enemy - his exact location, weaknesses, strengths, habits and preferences. Remember to remove the cause rather than treat the symptom. If you avoid the use and misuse of poison, you will avoid resistance and contamination problems, conserve beneficials, the environment and yourself.

Robert Metcalf, an entomologist, said, "The greatest single factor in preventing insects from overwhelming the rest of the world is the ... warfare which they carry out among themselves". Remember the old childhood riddle: The enemy of my enemy, is a friend of mine?

Rachael Carson said, "The second neglected fact is the truly explosive power of a species to reproduce once the resistance of the environment has been weakened". **The greatest weapon you have is your imagination - never depend on any one tool other than your brain and always seek a better, safer way!**

Even if the tool does not work - there are many, many others that will! Seek out knowledge with the same desire - you seek out the source and/or the pest - This manual will always need continual revision - there always will be one more safe, alternative pest control to try - rather than any dangerous, volatile poison! True IPM is not an acronym for "Include Pesticides Monthly" or "Increase Pesticide Marketing" or "Integrated Pesticide Management" - it stops the terrible poison "game" I call environmental roulette and it safely and far more effectively stops the pests!

ECOLOGICAL NARCOTICS - The use of volatile, synthetic pesticide poisons to "control or eliminate" pests is, obviously, not working. With any chemical dependency, routine use invariably makes worse the very problem it will supposedly eliminate, correct, control or fix. Using volatile pesticide poisons has not only created resistant pests, it has actually increased their numbers and damages and the severity of their attacks. Trying to drown one's sorrows in alcohol only creates bigger problems and greater sorrows and then even greater dependency and greater sorrow and problems. **It's time to get clean and sober!**

Definition of True IPM: Intelligent Pest Management® (IPM) is the coordinated use of pest and environmental information with available pest management methods to prevent unacceptable levels of pest damage by the most economical means, and with the least possible hazard to people and the environment. The goal of true IPM approach is to manage pests and the environment so as to balance costs, benefits, human health and environmental quality. True IPM systems utilize a high quantity and quality of technical information on the pest and its interaction with the environment (site). Because true IPM programs apply a holistic approach to pest management decision-making, they take advantage of all low risk management options, emphasizing natural biological methods, and the appropriate use of selective Pestisafes® and, as a last resort, selective, non-volatile, pesticides. True IPM's strategies incorporate environmental considerations by emphasizing pest management measures that minimize intrusion on natural bio-diversity ecosystems.

Thus, true IPM is:

- A system utilizing multiple methods that will not create resistance,
- A decision-making process,
- A risk reduction system,
- Information intensive,
- Biologically based,
- Safety conscious,
- Cost effective,
- Site specific and uses
- **Many alternatives to volatile, synthetic pesticide poisons.**

In over 350 schools, I have continually proven you do not need to use any volatile, "registered" pesticide poisons to safely and effectively control pest problems.

BREAKING THE CYCLE OF VIOLENCE - League of Women Voters

In our concern about "Breaking the Cycle of Violence," we do not want to overlook the neurotoxic and hormonal effects from many of the man-made chemicals that we are spewing into our environment. For example, "a very large proportion of all the pesticides used today are neurotoxic."[1] In experimenting with rats, Professor Warren Porter of the University of Wisconsin, Madison has found that tiny doses of combinations of pesticides (poisons), at levels that can be found in Wisconsin drinking water today, can cause both aggression and learning problems in the rats. He states, "Can you imagine any parents exposing their children to a toxic chemical? And yet they do it all the time [by pesticiding their homes and gardens, eating pesticided food, and permitting pesticiding in their children's schools and on their playgrounds].

The telling comparison is that we protect laboratory rats better from this stuff than we do our kids."[2] He said, "We will not be able to maintain a highly-ordered technological society if we raise a generation of children who are learning disabled and hyperaggressive."[3]

Many synthetic chemicals disrupt our hormones. Tiny doses can have devastating effects on the fetus, lasting a lifetime. Even although the genetic makeup of the individual can remain unchanged, the affected hormones control which genes will actually be expressed and in what way. Concerning these effects of man-made chemicals, the authors of Our Stolen Future write: "Wildlife data, laboratory experiments, the DES [a synthetic estrogen] experience, and a handful of human studies support the possibility of physical, mental, and behavioral disruption in humans that could affect fertility, learning ability, aggression, and conceivable even parenting and mating behavior. To what extent have scrambled [hormone] messages contributed to what we see happening around us - the reproductive problems seen among families and friends, the rash of learning problems showing up in our schools, the disintegration of the family and the neglect and abuse of children, and the increasing violence in our society?"[4]

1. Young, B. B., "Neurotoxicity of Pesticides," Journal of Pesticide Reform, 6(2): 6, summer 1986.
2. Knapp, Dan, "Warning! Good Looking Lawns May Be Hazardous to Your Health," On Wisconsin, page 53, May/June 1996.
3. Telephone conversation between Marjorie Fisher and Professor Warren P. Porter, Chair, Wisconsin, Madison, March 5, 1991.
4. Colborn, Theo, Dianne Dumanoski, and John Peterson Myers, Our Stolen Future, Are We Threatening Our Fertility, Intelligence, and Survival? — A Scientific Story, Dutton, 1996, page 232.

Michigan Living, March 1998, Volume 80, No. 6, noted that studies at AAA show the number of aggressive driving incidents has risen 51% since 1990. This study specifically measured only the number of times a driver tries to kill or injure another after a traffic dispute. The study did not note the increased amount of verbal abuse or obscene gestures which we now all have to deal with daily.

Helen Keller was once asked, "Is there anything worse than not having your sight?" She responded earnestly, "Oh, yes; it would be much worse to have your sight but not to have vision!"

Enough of the problems - On with the answers and the vision!

BITING, STINGING AND/OR BLOOD FEEDERS OVERVIEW

Have You Just Been Bitten or Stung?

What you don't know can hurt you.

When it comes to bites and stings - prevention is your best medicine.

What can you do?
First, learn which creatures can bite or sting.
Next, understand what you can do to avoid a problem.
Last, know what to do and whom to call if you get bitten or stung.

How toxic are the venoms of stinging ants, bees and wasps? As Justin Schmidt noted: The sting of a tiny fire ant, which weights in at about three billionth of an ounce, can have a terrific impact on a huge person that weights about 10 million times as much as the ant. About 70,000 species of Hymenoptera (ants, bees, wasps, etc.) can sting. I like to note only the females can sting you. We are all different and unique so we may only experience a little pain, or we may experience extreme pain and allergic reaction. **Avoid being stung if at all possible!**

How many Texans have felt the "sting" of fire ants? A Winter 2000 poll conducted 2/9-25/00 by the Scripps Howard Data Center noted 79% of all polled Texans had been stung by fire ants and a majority of the residents had been treated for them in the past year. West Texans were least likely to have been stung (61%) as opposed to Central Texans (90%). Eastern Texans had been stung 89%, Southern Texans were stung 78% and 72% of Northern Texans that were polled noted they had been stung by fire ants. Of the Texans over 60 years old that were stung, 68% were treated, as compared to 37% of the 18 to 29 year olds that were stung by fire ants. Among those treated for fire ant stings, 51% were treated 4 or more times. The margin for error for the whole sample is + or - 3 percentage points, and slightly larger for the subgroups. **I would like to add the best repellent for fire ants I have found is baby powder with talcum. No matter how much volatile pesticide poison "they" spray, the spray ants continually are increasing in numbers and in infested territory!**

Help is simply a phone call away. If you are bitten or stung, call your local health care provider or physician to determine if you can be treated at home, need to be seen by a physician or should go directly to a hospital emergency department. If you can be treated at home, your health care provider should keep in phone contact with you by calling back and checking on your condition. If your condition worsens, you should go to the nearest emergency department or call the paramedics or an ambulance. **The following suggestions are not intended to replace proper medical care. Always treat a small area before using any product, herb, oil, shampoo, soap, cleaner or material on your body.**

Things you can do to prevent venomous bites or stings:

(It helps if you do not look or smell like a flower or wear flashy jewelry.)

When hiking

- ☺ Wear plain, light-colored clothing: long, heavy pants, long sleeves, netting and high-top, lace-up leather shoes or boots that cover the ankles.
- ☺ Watch out for snakes and stinging insects. Be extra cautious when daytime temperatures stay over 82_o F. Snake encounters are more likely on south sides of slopes and hills.
- ☺ Use a walking stick - it can be a good hiking companion. It can be used in an emergency to help avoid a snake or creature.
- ☺ Carefully look around rocks or logs before stepping down.
- ☺ Watch for bee hives, colonies
- ☺ Don't wave at, yell at, handle, annoy, touch or try to play with wild animals, spiders, stinging insects, snakes or Gila monsters. Walk around them if you can.

When camping - or at home -

- ☺ Check and shake bedding, clothes, boots and shoes before use.
- ☺ Do not leave any food around that is not tightly sealed in glass. Food odors attract insects and wildlife.
- ☺ Close and zip and then duct tape all tent closures during the

or swarms when outdoors – Don't poke at or touch them.

- ☺ Don't place your hands where you can't see.
- ☺ Be very cautious under rocks or logs.

night.

- ☺ Be aware that during the hot summer months rattlesnakes are more active and hunt at night.
- ☺ Keep a good first aid kid with you. A snake bite kit is usually not necessary.

THINGS YOU CAN DO TO PREVENT VENOMOUS BITES OR STINGS AROUND YOUR HOME:

- ☺ Get rid of rocks, mulch, litter, wood, paper, logs and debris from your yard.
- ☺ Wear plain, light-colored and long sleeved clothing, heavy work gloves, high top boots and long pants when working outside around your yard.
- ☺ Keep doors and windows tight fitting with good weather stripping.
- ☺ Make sure other openings (such as where air cond-itioners, swamp coolers or exhaust fans enter your house) are closed, sealed or fitted with a fine mesh screen and are dusted with talcum powder.
- ☺ Fill all cracks in the foundation of the house and around all water faucets.
- ☺ Look before you place your hand under or into something, especially rocks.
- ☺ Make periodic checks for bee hives or swarms; if found, carefully follow the directions in The Best Control© or The Best Control II©.
- ☺ Be very careful when operating vibrating equipment (lawn mowers, chain saws, weed eaters, etc.) that may disturb a fire ant, bee hive or wasp nest.
- ☺ Carefully check all line-dried clothing prior to bringing any of it inside the house.
- ☺ Do not leave shoes, boots, drinks, clothing items and towels outdoors.
- ☺ Always protect your feet and wear shoes when outdoors, night
- ☺ Don't aggravate stinging insects that approach you.
- ☺ Always check your clothing, bed and footwear before getting in them.
- ☺ For help in removing snakes or other venomous creatures from your property, read The Best Control© or The Best Control II©. Call 1-800-221-6188 to order your CD-ROM copy.

Repellants - Bathing in a tub of warm water with 2 capfuls of chlorine bleach can repel insects, arachnids and/or mites for hours. Certain bath oils, Noxema®, Vicks Vaporub® and/or some sunscreens also can repel pests. Thiamine chloride (a B vitamin) taken orally or 60 milligrams of zinc taken daily also will act as a natural repellant.

Rattlesnakes

Rattlesnakes have a flattened, triangular shaped head with a heat-sensing device located between the nostril and eye on each side that is used to locate and trail prey. Different species of rattlesnakes can be of different lengths, with the Western Diamondback growing up from 10 inches at birth to 6 feet in length. The most common rattlesnakes include the Western Diamondback, Mohave, Sidewinder, Black- tailed, Speckled and Tiger. Rattlesnake bites are rarely fatal but can be extremely painful. Caution and common sense should be used. Most bites happen when you accidentally or purposely disturb or handle or play with the snake. It's far better to walk around or avoid it. Extra caution should be taken, especially when daytime temperature stays above 82o F. or 28o C. Baby rattlesnakes are typically born at the end of July and can bite at birth. The shaking of the rattle can serve as a warning but rattlesnakes can strike without warning or making any sound. They can strike ¼ to ½ of their body length. Coloring varies by species, but most blend with their environments, so they are extremely hard to see. **If you must kill them, wear protective clothing and use a shovel to decapitate them. Remember, even a severed head can still strike and kill!**

General Signs and Symptoms of a Snake Bites

- ☹ Immediate pain or a burning sensation generally will occur at the site of the bite.
- ☹ Fang marks are usually visible.
- ☹ A metallic or rubbery taste in the mouth.
- ☹ Significant swelling within minutes.
- ☹ Muscle weakness, sweating and/or chills, nausea and vomiting.

Note: A small percentage of rattlesnake bites are "dry," meaning that the snake has not injected venom. **But always seek medical help immediately**. Remember, protocols may vary from one hospital to another, so ask for the newest treatment. The venom injected contains several enzymes designed to attack tissue damage. The venom may also contain components that cause blood thinning and other effects on the body. The average cost to treat a venomous snake bite can be between $15,000 and $20,000 without medical complications, but almost half of the treated bites can become complicated, e.g., an allergic reaction to horse-based sera or to the venom itself. 95% of snake bites occur below the knees or below the elbows, so protect yourself!

Treatment

- ☹ *Don't* apply ice to the bite site or immerse the bite in a bucket of ice.
- ☹ *Don't* use a constricting band/cloth or tourniquet. Do not restrict blood flow in any manner.
- ☹ *Don't* cut the bite site or try to suck out the venom. Leave the bite site alone!
- ☹ *Don't* use electric shock or stun guns of any kind.
- ☹ *Don't* try to capture the snake to bring it to the hospital.
- ☺ *Do*, if you are not sensitive, take 2 - 3 droppers full of tincture of echinacea every hour for up to 12 hours in order to quickly activate the immune system.
- ☺ *Do* take high doses of vitamin C for its beneficial anti-allergy and antihistamine effects.
- ☺ *Do* use chewed crushed plantain leaves as they have antiinflammatory, antitoxic and antibacterial effects.

Seek medical help from a hospital emergency room or physician immediately. Back away quickly to prevent being bitten again. Identify the snake if you can. Rinse the bite area. Clean with soap and water or an antiseptic; apply a bandage or clean cloth. Remove constrictive items. Monitor for allergic reaction and/or shock. If possible and safe, remove venom. Keep victim as calm, relaxed and quiet as possible. Immobilize and splint the bitten extremity and then keep it below heart level. Don't allow the victim to drink alcohol, eat food or take any medications. You need to be evaluated and perhaps be administered antivenin. Move slowly if necessary to get help. You have time to reach medical care. Don't panic. Stay as calm as possible. If bitten on the hand, remove all jewelry before swelling begins. You can take echinacea internally and externally. Take high doses of vitamin C. Freshly crushed or chewed plantain leaves can be applied as a poultice. You can also make a daily poultice of echinacea, comfrey and/or calendula.

Lizard Bites from Gila Monsters

This large, heavy-bodied lizard displays contrasting markings of pink, yellow, orange and black. It measures up to 2 feet long and weights up to 2 pounds. It is the only venomous lizard in the United States, and it is a shy creature. Bites usually only happen when it is cornered or picked up. The Gila monster prefers canyon bottoms, rocky areas and outlying desert residential areas. It spends less than 2 weeks per year above ground. From early March to mid-May, Gila monsters are active during the day and this changes to nighttime beginning with the monsoons.

Signs and Symptoms of a Gila Monster Bite

A bite produces intense pain within 30 seconds, followed by swelling, weakness, dizziness, nausea and chills.

Treatment

Once a Gila monster bites, it does not generally let go. Therefore, you or someone with you may have to pull it off. The longer it remains on you, the more venomous the bite. Once off, wash the bite site with soap and water or an antiseptic to help remove some of the venom from the bite site. Apply ice or cold compresses to the area to help keep the venom localized. Do not wait for symptoms to occur: go to the closest medical facility or physician for treatment.

Scorpions

All U. S. scorpions can sting, but only the bark scorpion normally can cause serious medical problems. It chooses to live in well defined geographic areas. The small bark scorpion only measures from 1 to 1-½ inches in length. Its color varies from light tan to a dark golden brown. It also is the only scorpion that curls its tail to the side while at rest.

A nighttime feeder, it is most commonly found near irrigated areas, pools, in palm trees, concrete block fences and wooden fences and on the walls in homes. The bark scorpion is the only scorpion that can climb walls and walk across ceilings. It, therefore, can show up in bathtubs, sinks and beds, having fallen from the ceiling. It also has the ability to cling to the underside of wood, making it important to be extremely cautious when handling wood or outdoor furniture. Many times scorpions are found in cupboards, showers and other unexpected places. Scorpions are most active when the daytime temperatures are 70_{o} F. or above.

Special Precautions

Because children under 10 years old are more likely to develop severe symptoms if stung by a scorpion, special care should be taken if you are visiting or reside in a bark scorpion-prone area:

- ☺ To prevent scorpions from either climbing or falling into the crib, place netting over the crib and place the crib legs in clean, wide-mouth jars or wrap with duct tape, sticky-side out.
- ☺ Place duct tape sticky-side up and secured with (masking) tape on the edges along the edges of walls and/or around the bed and/or furniture.
- ☺ Roll back bed linens and carefully inspect for scorpions before getting into bed.

- ☺ Shake and examine all clothing and shoes before putting them on.
- ☺ Move furniture and beds away from the walls.
- ☺ No bare feet; always wear shoes when outdoors, especially around a pool at night.
- ☺ Be especially careful of wet/damp towels in the bathroom and pool area.

Signs and Symptoms of a Scorpion Sting

In infants and children watch for excessive crying, rapid, jittery or uncoordinated eye movements and increased drooling or saliva. They constantly rub their noses and faces, indicating facial numbness, tingling and visual disturbances. Bark scorpion stings can cause one or several of the following symptoms, usually within the first 2 - 3 hours following the sting:

- ☹ Immediate local pain/burning/prickly sensation. **No swelling or redness.**
- ☹ The site of the sting is very sensitive; a slight touch causes great pain.
- ☹ Numbness and tingling moves from the sting site to distant body parts.
- ☹ Difficulty swallowing and "swollen tongue" sensation with excessive drooling.
- ☹ Slurred speech.
- ☹ Muscle twitching.
- ☹ Restlessness and irritability.
- ☹ Respiratory problems with possible respiratory arrest.

Treatment

Call your medical provider to determine whether the sting victim can be managed at home or will require medical treatment, e.g., intravenous medication to relieve muscle pain and spasm. **If in doubt, go to the emergency room.** Garlic has been used to relieve scorpion stings. It is thought the sulfur components help neutralize the toxins.

Black Widow Spiders

A mature female black widow spider has a large, black, shiny body and measures approximately 3/8 inch long, with 1inch legs. An hourglass shape in bright red or orange-red color can be found on the abdomen. Black widow spider webs are very irregular, not in lively concentric rings; they are white and very strong. They are most often found in areas where water and insects are readily available. Around the home they can be found under or in outdoor furniture, barbecue grills, pool pumps and in storage areas, garages, wood piles, block fences and the corners of porches and patios.

The black widow is shy. She hides near the web by day and is most active at night where she waits in her web for prey to enter. She produces hundreds of babies hatched from egg sacs that look like little moth balls. The young black widows are white in color and spread quickly after hatching. The male black widow is much smaller and is brown and white in color. Because of its size, its bite cannot pierce skin and is, therefore, not dangerous to humans.

Black Widow Spider Control

A "live and let live" attitude is the best approach for living in harmony with all nature. But if you have a problem of close contact with the black widow or you have young children who play outside, you may have to take steps to control the black widow population around your house. To control the black widow populations, locate the black widow spider, using a flashlight at night to find her in her web; then vacuum her and her web and her eggs up and safely dispose of the bag.

Signs and Symptoms of a Black Widow Spider Bite

The initial bite may feel like a tiny prick and may go unnoticed. At first, there may be little or no visible signs of the bite such as swelling. A red circular mark may appear about 6 hours after the bite. The symptoms may progress to aching sensations, muscle pain at the bite site spreading to the lower back, thighs and limbs. A black widow spider bite can cause intense abdominal pain that can be confused with appendicitis. Symptoms can last 36 hours and lingering effects may last for several weeks.

Treatment

Keep the bite site lower than the level of the victim's heart and clean the wound/bite site with alcohol or a moist aspirin or soap and water. Then apply ice or cold packs to the bitten area to slow the circulation of the venom. Remove rings or constricting items since the bitten area may swell. Never cut or suction a spider bite. Keep the victim quiet and watch for signs of shock. Call your medical provider immediately to determine whether the bite victim can be managed at home or will require treatment by a physician or hospitalization. Several cases may require antivenin treatment.

Africanized Honey Bees (Killer Bees)

The Africanized honey bee looks the same as the European honey bee, but is much more aggressive in defending its hives or colonies and can attack without warning. One or even hundreds of bees target the head in an attack. A single sting is no more powerful or painful than that of the European honey bee, but killer bee victims can be stung hundreds of times. If attacked, cover your head and run in a zigzag pattern and find shelter in a building or car or dark area as quickly as possible. Then quickly remove all stingers from the skin. **Get emergency medical help immediately.**

European Honey Bees

The European honey bee pollinates crops and flowers. It is about 1 inch long and is colored golden brown with black strips encircling its fuzzy abdomen. A honey bee's venom is just as dangerous as that of a rattlesnake, only there is less toxin involved in a single sting. So it is vital to remove the poison sac as soon as possible. After a sting, the barbed stinger remains in the skin with the venom sac attached. Do not attempt to pull out the stinger with your fingers because as you squeeze, you force more venom into your body. Instead, use a piece of hard plastic (credit card) or fingernail to scrape or flick the stinger out of the skin. Bees are more easily agitated on cloudy days, or by dark or bright clothing, or by vibrations or loud noises. Bees typically attack the head and ankles. 100 - 200 stings can be fatal to an average adult. The venom from a dozen stings can cause rapid onset of swelling, headache, muscle cramps and fever. **If you have been stung multiple times or are experiencing any allergic reactions, e.g., swelling in other parts of the body, breathing problems, chest construction, abdominal cramps or shock, get emergency medical help immediately. If attacked, see above.**

Ants

Many ants can sting or bite and use their venom to kill smaller creatures or to keep intruders away. Therefore, the best prevention is to avoid stepping on or sitting on all of their nests.

Wasps

Wasps are slender with a relatively thin waist and four wings. Smooth and somewhat shiny, wasps have brightly colored "skin," often with sharply contrasting black and yellow patterns. Females can sting multiple times. The males have wings but no stingers. Wasps are beneficial predators and feed on insects and spiders. Because its stinger is not barbed, it can be removed and reinserted repeatedly, each time injecting out enough venom to cause considerable pain.

Yellow jackets have jagged bands of yellow and black. The stings are painful and they attack viciously outdoors when nests are bothered.

Signs and Symptoms of Bee, Ant or Wasp Stings

The severity of an insect sting reaction varies from person to person. A normal reaction will result in pain, swelling and redness around the sting site. A large local reaction includes swelling and redness beyond the sting site. Although frightening in appearance, these large local reactions usually will go away over several days. The most serious reaction to any insect bite or sting is an allergic one. Any of these reactions requires immediate medical attention. Symptoms of a severe allergic reaction or "anaphylaxis" may include one or more of the following:

- ☹ Redness, hives, itching or swelling in areas other than the sting/bite site.
- ☹ Tightness in or constriction of the chest and difficulty breathing.
- ☹ Abdominal cramps.
- ☹ Hoarse voice or swelling of the tongue.
- ☹ Dizziness or a sharp drop in blood pressure.
- ☹ Unconsciousness, shock or cardiac arrest.
- ☹ **Delayed reactions can also occur.**

This type of reaction can occur within minutes after the sting/bite and may be life-threatening. People who have previously experienced an allergic reaction to an insect sting or bite have a good chance of a similar or worse reaction if stung or bitten again by the same kind of insect. If you have severe allergies to any insect, always carry appropriate medicine prescribed by your physician with you when you go outdoors. To relieve minor stings or itches, apply a paste of baking soda and water, half of a cut onion, apple cider vinegar or meat tenderizer or a moist aspirin to the sting/bite. **Remember that baking soda is alkaline and will neutralize the acidic stings of bees and that vinegar is an acid and will help soothe the alkaline sting of a wasp. See treatment below.**

Treatment

Wash the sting/bite site with soap and water or an antiseptic to help remove some of the venom from the skin's surface. Apply cold compresses to the site to help keep the venom localized. Have the victim rest. Apply freshly chewed or crushed plantain leaves to the site or apply a paste of warm water and powdered bentonite clay or activated charcoal to the site. You can also ingest a few capsules of activated charcoal. Other products that have helped people relieve bee stings are honey, lemon, lime, onion, papaya, vinegar, Swedish bitters, cold milk compresses, baking soda, a moist aspirin, essential oil of lavender, vitamin B, fresh aloe, vitamin C paste, witch hazel, meat tenderizer and/or enzyme cleaners or Not Nice to Itching™ or, in a pinch, a mud pack. Call your health care provider to determine whether the bite can be managed at home or will require medical treatment. If you are bitten or stung and did not see the insect, call your health care provider. From the symptoms you describe, the nurses or doctors will determine if your bite or sting could be poisonous and if you need to be examined by a doctor.

Arizona Brown Spiders (Fiddleback Spiders)

This small brown spider does have the potential to be venomous. Brown spiders are about the size of a half-dollar, including legs, and are distinguished by a violin or "fiddle" marking on the back of the head. This timid arthropod produces an irregular web. It tends to live in the foothills or desert areas that are dry, littered and undisturbed. There it may seek shelter in garages, wood, dead cactus, pack rat nests, storage areas or trash undisturbed. There it may seek shelter in garages, wood, dead cactus, pack rat nests, storage areas or trash piles. On rare occasions it may be found in bedding or clothing - but again, only in desert-situated settings. If you believe you have been bitten by an Arizona brown spider, try to capture it and bring it with you to the medical facility. Call your health care provider to determine whether the bite victim can be managed at home or will require medical treatment.

Brown Recluse Spiders

The brown recluse spider is shy, sedentary and builds an irregular web that is often not even recognized as a spider web. Females lay eggs in flattened egg sacs that are frequently attached to the underside of objects. Mating in this species occurs from February to September. Up to 40 spiderlings may hatch from a single egg sac. A single female may produce up to five egg sacs in a summer. Females can live up to four years, males less.

Indoors, the brown recluse can usually be found in infrequently disturbed areas away from light sources, such as behind pictures, beneath or behind furniture, in boxes, in clothing, among stored papers, between the corrugation of boxes, under food sacks and behind old boards leaning against walls.

The natural habitat of the brown recluse includes the underside of rocks, loose bark and crevices in decaying logs (Hite et al. 1966). However, many outdoor hiding areas provided by the activities of man are frequently inhabited by the brown recluse spider. For example, a survey of piles of junk in Kansas, piles of old tires and inner tubes, furniture, old boards and trash were found to be inhabited by the brown recluse. Once the debris/harborage was removed and the natural vegetation returned to the area, the colony was eliminated. There are at least 13 species in the U. S.

Signs of a Brown Recluse Bite

Brown Recluse bites are sharp but not initially painful like those of the Black Widow, but a small, white blister is quickly raised, broken, and surrounded by a red welt. An hour or more may pass; then there may be intense pain. The depressed center of this raised, red circle (the size of a dime to a quarter) turns dark within a day. The dead tissue regularly sloughs away, and the bite area scars over in one to eight weeks. Death seldom occurs, but the bite is debilitating and psychologically traumatic. Note: A bite from a brown recluse may also produce an intensely sore lump, even several weeks after the initial injury.

Treatment

Seek medical attention immediately. Keep the bite site lower than the level of the victim's heart and wash the wound with alcohol or a moist aspirin, soap and water. Then apply ice or cold compresses to try to slow the circulation of the venom. Keep the victim quiet and watch for signs of shock. **See a health professional.**

Conenose Bugs (Kissing Bugs)

This slow-moving bug is dark brown to black with yellow/red markings on the abdomen and measures ½ to 1 inch long. Its body is long with 3 pairs of legs and a cone-shaped head. The conenose bug usually bites and feeds on the blood of its victim when the victim is asleep. Seen in the spring and early summer, it makes its home inside rodent and bird nests. During the day it may hide indoors under furniture or in closets. Put down duct tape, sticky side up and held down with (masking) tape, on the edges to trap these pests.

Signs and Symptoms of a Conenose Bug Bite

The bite can be painful with redness, swelling and itching. Each time a bite takes place, the victim becomes more sensitive. Each bite can then cause a serious allergic reaction that causes itching scalp, palms and soles, welts or rash, nausea, vomiting and breathing problems. Anaphylactic reaction can occur in very sensitive people.

Call your health care provider to determine whether the bite victim can be managed at home or will require medical treatment. If possible, capture the bug in order to confirm the bite was that of a conenose bug.

Ticks

If you do not wish to wear any repellant, wear light colored clothing and tuck pants into socks or tape them to the legs tightly. Leave as little skin exposed as possible. If you are in a tick infested area, inspect hourly for ticks, especially between the ankle and the knee. Have someone help you check your entire body at noon and at bedtime after you shower and before you go to bed. Be extremely careful when you inspect the head, back, groin and armpits. Remember: An engorged nymph will only be the size of a poppy seed. If any ticks are found on you or your pet, don't kill them; cover them with Vaseline, melted wax or fingernail polish. May be they will back out on their own or suffocate. If they don't, take a pair of tweezers, gently pull them out with a slow, steady pressure. Don't twist. Once the tick has been removed, drop it into a plastic pill bottle with alcohol to kill it and then wash the bite site with soap and water and then apply iodine or another antiseptic. Save the tick and call your doctor for further advice. Wash all clothing in borax and put all other non-washable materials in a clothes dryer - the dryer's temperature will kill all ticks.

Unknown Bites and Stings

If you are bitten or stung and did not see the insect or creature, wash the area with soap and water or a moist aspirin or an antiseptic and call your health care provider immediately, especially if you experience any discomfort. From the symptoms you describe, the nurse or doctor can normally determine if your bite or sting could be poisonous or serious and if you need to be personally examined by a doctor.

Treatment of Minor Animal Bites

- Wash the bite with soap and water to remove saliva and any other contamination.
- Tincture of calendula or echinacea can be diluted 5 to 1 with warm water to disinfect the site.
- Essential oil of tea tree or lavender can be added at a rate of 6 - 8 drops per cup of warm water or put a drop right on the wound or bandage. Oils get into the blood stream quickly.
- Open the wound and pour in some 3% hydrogen peroxide until it foams up.
- Plantain leaves can be chewed or crushed into a slippery mass and then applied to minor bites and wounds. Apply ice and elevate the area if there is any swelling; to stop bleeding elevate the area above the heart level and cover the entire wound with a clean cloth and press it firmly against the wound.
- Call and/or see your medical care provider as soon as possible.

Note: If you are not sensitive, a dropper full of tincture of echinacea can also be given internally every hour for three hours for minor animal bites. Before treatment with any material, be sure you are not sensitive to it.

BLOOD FEEDING ARTHROPODS GENERAL DESCRIPTION

Blood feeding anthropod pests are of great concern not only because of their annoying and often painful bites, but more importantly because many can also be vectors (carriers) of pathogenic (disease) organisms, that seriously injure or kill humans and domestic animals, e.g., encephalitis, tularema, Lyme disease, malaria, yellow fever, Chaga's disease, bubonic plague, murine typhus, tapeworms, Rocky Mountain fever, etc. Specific identification is particularly critical in these dangerous pests because members of each group are very similar in appearance, but differ in their choice of hosts, habits and potential as disease vectors.

Every blood feeder needs a blood meal at some point to complete its life cycle. The only exception are some of the males of this group, e.g., male mosquitoes, male horse flies, etc., who don't need blood. Some blood feeders will feed on only one host species. However, most blood feeders have not only a preferred host, but also will feed on a wide range of substitute hosts. When multiple host species are involved, there is a greater possibility of disease transmission, e.g., the malarial parasite, yellow fever virus, rickettsiae of Rocky Mountain spotted fever, the bubonic plague bacillus, etc. Many wild animals can serve as reservoirs of disease organisms and still suffer only a few or no ill effects themselves, e.g., roof rats are reservoirs for human plague and typhus with fleas serving as the vectors of these diseases. Some of these blood feeders remind us we are not always on the top of every food chain.

1. **First, properly locate and identify** the blood-feeding pest(s) involved.
2. **Second, practice exclusion and prevention.** This consists of denying access into the structure of the hosts and the insects themselves. Access to any crawl spaces or attics must be denied so wild animals such as opossums, feral cats and dogs, skunks, birds, bats, commensal rodents, squirrels and raccoons cannot enter. Exclusion consists of reducing openings into the building so that wild animals and/or insects cannot gain entrance. This is done by carefully plugging or sealing holes with concrete, caulk or other appropriate material; carefully screening windows, doors and vents; reducing door threshold gaps, installing doorsweeps, installing negative ion plates, spraying enzyme cleaners, mopping with borax, etc.
3. **Indoor control and sanitation**. Mechanically reduce pests by vacuuming or steam cleaning or rinse-and-vacuuming all rugs, floors and fabric-covered furniture along with routine cleaning or properly disposing of all infested pet bedding. Remove and clean up all harborage debris; vacuum or steam all insects, spiders and/or mites; remove all rodent nests; caulk all cracks

and crevices; vent and cover all crawls; routinely and thoroughly clean with Kleen 'Em Away Naturally® or Safe Solutions, Inc. Enzyme Cleaners or Peppermint Soap and/or borax.

4. **Outdoor control**. Begin with sanitation, e.g., debris removal; keep the grass and weeds mowed; trim all branches that touch or overhang the building; remove all old bird nests from the structure, and eliminate any alternate hosts and their harborage within 100 yards of the structure. Sanitation is followed by the application of diluted Kleen 'Em Away Naturally® or Safe Solutions, Inc. ((protease) enzyme cleaners or peppermint soap or other Pestisafes®, e.g., talcum powder, food-grade diatomaceous earth (DE), peppermint soap, Vaseline, freshly ground pepper, menthol rub and/or Tide® soap. Application may range from spot application along the exterior foundation wall and adjacent perimeter band treatment to whole yard treatment depending on the **imminent** danger to humans. Wettable powder and microencapsulated pesticide formulations can be effective, **if absolutely necessary**, but as in the case of **all** volatile, synthetic pesticide poison poisons there is an obvious risk of contamination of wells, air, pets and people whenever they are used. Be sure there is **no** other alternative and **all** Pestisafes® have been tried first!
5. **The best treatment for insect bites and stings is to avoid them in the first place.** If practical, wear 2 layers of clothing, avoid floral prints, hair spray, perfumes and shiny jewelry. The color blue is the preferred color of mosquitoes; wear white, tan and/or light green clothing. Routinely shower with pepper- mint soap. Try orally taking 3 - 4 garlic capsules and vitamin B and nutritional yeast daily. Avoid eating sugars, alcohol, tropical fruits and juices. Thread a sprig of elder through your hair. To create a mosquito-free environment, boil willow in water, burn artemesia in a campfire or diffuse various combina- tions of the oils of citronella, eucalyptus, pennyroyal, grape seed, almond, lavender, rosemary, tea tree, basil, geranium and/or sage into the areas. You can also make a room spray with water and a few drops of these essential oils or with enzymes. Essential oils, e.g., geraniol or geranium oil and coconut oil, diluted in olive oil or aloe vera nectar or jojoba can be applied topically to pulse points on your body every hour or so to repel insects (e.g., fire ants, ticks, fleas, mosquitoes, lice and gnats), but can be irritating to some people, **so always test them on a small area of your skin first!** As the odor lessens, so does the effectiveness. Try chamomile tea, thyme, sweet basil, yarrow, vanilla extract or try dilutions of camphor, tea tree, bergamot, patchouli, sandalwood, peppermint oil, Guatemalan lemon grass, lavender, cedar wood and pennyroyal *(Mentha pulegium)*

individually or as blends. Pennyroyal's Latin name means mint and flea and the plant and smoke from its burning leaves help control these pests, but avoid mint plants if you are pregnant or sensitive. Other essential oils that can be made and used as repellents include menthol, citronella, eucalyptus, geranium and okra but they can stain clothing; do not drink them and be careful around your eyes and mouth when applying them.

6. If bitten, leave the area immediately, and if the bite is considered serious, go to a physician immediately, but first remove the stinger and cleanse the area as soon as possible. If you are not sensitive, you can ingest homeopathic *Apis mellifica* and rub an apis-based cream or a little epsom salt water or enzyme cleaner on the wound every 15 minutes until relief arrives. You can also apply echinacea tincture to the sting area and take it internally to help reduce allergic reactions and other immunological disturbances. If the bite/sting feels better when cold is applied or the area is already cold and/or numb, use homeopathic ledum. Ice alleviates pain and swelling and mud or clay, fresh garlic, onion juice, witch hazel, baking soda or meat tenderizer paste eases itching and aching. (Baking soda is an alkali that neutralizes acid. Applied to the skin it acts to reduce pain and swelling, draws out toxins and helps neutralize some of the inflammatory agents in the toxins.) Meat tenderizer is made from papain, a protease enzyme derived from papaya and helps break down the inflammatory properties of venom. (That is why protease enzyme cleaners and shampoos also work.) Various herbs rubbed into insect bites may also accelerate healing: ground-up comfrey, sweet basil, tea tree oil (a powerful wound healer and germicide), olive oil, marigold, yellow dock, wild marjoram, leek bulbs, crushed parsley or plantain and/or the leaves of rue, St. John's wort, plantain, house leek, aloe and pennyroyal. Apply calendula petals on a bee sting. Wasp stings are best treated with any wild mallow flower or freshly chewed or crushed plantain leaves, slices of onion or garlic or vinegar applied topically, accompanied by an internal dose of homeopathic vespa. Taking vitamin C and panthothenic acid over a period of 3 - 4 hours helps create a natural antihistamine effect, thus reducing swelling. The enzymes bromelain and quercitin also help reduce inflammation. If you are upset try taking a calming flower remedy under the tongue every 10 minutes until you settle down. If you are allergic to bee stings, get medical attention immediately. Your own urine on a cloth has antibodies that can neutralize an insect's venom. Apply pulped or crushed leaves of wormwood, rue or sage to alleviate the pain of scorpions, spiders or jellyfish, but some people may be sensitive, especially to wormwood or rue. Increase your intake of vitamin C and you receive anti-inflammatory effects and boost your liver's ability to filter out the toxins. Take chlorophyll supplements to boost your immune system and help detoxify your blood. Take shiitake or reishi mushroom supplements to help you detoxify. **Try spraying a mix of 1000 mg. of vitamin C in a cup of warm water (a 1% - 3% solution) or diluted Kleen 'Em Away Naturally® or Safe Solutions, Inc. Enzyme Cleaner from a small "spritzer" bottle on the bite/sting as a sting reliever. Seek medical attention.**

7. Bend the arm and note where it forms a crease at the elbow. Put your thumb at the point at the end of the crease, away from the body and press slowly into the joint. This accupressure point helps alleviate the redness and swelling of bites and stings.
8. Remember, the emotional reaction to a sting or bite is often more severe than the actual hazard from the venom.

Just a few alternatives to synthetic pesticide poisons:

1. **Neem** - One of the best natural or botanical pesticides for controlling bloodfeeding arthropods and other pests is Neem. **What is Neem?** Neem, a member of the *Meliaceae* family and a botanical cousin of mahogany, is a tall, fast-growing, evergreen tree which has an attractive crown of deep-green leaves and masses of honey-scented flowers and thrives even in nutrient-poor, dry soil. It tolerates high temperatures, low rainfall, long spells of drought and salinity, and can be propagated by seed. Because of its many benefits, neem has been worshipped as a goddess in India. Neem is bitter in taste. The bitterness is due to the presence of an array of complex compounds called "triterpenes" or more specifically "liminoids". The most important bioactive principle is a terpenoid known as azadirachtin; however, at least 10 other neem limonoids also possess insect growth regulating activity. The tree's scientific name is *Azadiractita indica.* Neem has been used for centuries primarily against household and storage pests, and to a limited extent against crop pests. Neem trees were the only green thing left standing during a ravaging locust plague in Sudan in 1959. Neem does not kill pests but affects their behavior and physiology and reduces the risk of exposing the pests' natural enemies to poisoned food sources or starvation. Neem derivatives affect more than 200 insect species belonging to *Coleoptera, Diptera, Heteroptera, Homoptera, Hymenoptera, Lepidoptera, Orthoptera, Thysanoptera,* several species of mites and nematodes, and even noxious snails and fungi. Although neem oil can be used directly for pest control, semi-

purified "bitters" and "neem rich" fractions can easily be standardized for biological properties and could satisfy even stringent quality requirements. Being water soluble, they also can be applied as systemic compounds which render them more photostable and nonphytotoxic. A garlic odor often present in other neem products is absent in "bitters". Neem products are effective and relatively hazard-free. An added benefit of using semi-purified neem fractions, rather than pure compounds, is that pests will be less likely to develop resistance. Neem compounds act together on several different behavioral and physiological processes which also helps prevent insects from evolving resistance to the compound. Their effects include repellence, feeding deterrence, reduced ingestion and digestion of food, poor growth and development, reduced longevity and fecundity, mating disruption, oviposition deterrence, inhibition of egg hatchability, molting failures and direct toxicity. Reports suggest that by paralyzing the muscles in the insects' mandibles neem induces starvation. At lower than lethal dozes, azadirachtin also mimics juvenile hormone, preventing insects from maturing. Neem-based insecticides can be further fortified against dynamic pests by optimizing their use with microbials or other botanicals. Neem fruits, seeds, oil, leaves, bark and roots can be used as general antiseptics, antimicrobials for the treatment of urinary disorders, diarrhea, fever, bronchitis, skin diseases, septic sores, infected burns, hypertension and inflammatory diseases. Neem oil and its isolates - nimbidin, nimbidol and nimbin - inhibit fungal growth on humans and animals. Neem leaf extracts and teas are used to treat malaria; ioquin tablets and injections containing neem extract are currently being formulated for treating chronic malaria. Exposing kissing bugs *(Rhodnius prolixus),* the major vector of Chagas disease in Latin America, to neem extracts or to azadirachtin "immu*prolixus),* the major vector of Chagas disease in Latin America, to neem extracts or to azadirachtin "immunizes" them against their internal protozoan parasite *Trypanosoma cruzi*. We are trying it on termites. Cattle leaf supplements containing neem leaf powder are used as worm killers. Creams containing neem oil are used for animal wound dressing and also act as fly and mosquito repellents. Neem oil in human bathing and laundry soap kills lice and neem in dog soaps and shampoos controls ticks and fleas. Neem twigs are used daily by millions in Bangladesh, India and Pakistan as disposable toothbrushes; extracts of neem bark are used in some toothpastes and mouthwashes. Neem plantings also serve as a refuge for honeybees, wasps, spiders, birds, bats and other beneficial organisms, and the litter of falling leaves can improve soil fertility. Neem overall as a relatively safe, natural (botanical) pesticide poison with numerous benefits. Neem nectar does not kill pollinating bees.

2. **Noxema®** - We have found that Noxema® or Ben-Gay® applied to the exposed skin of children and people repels mosquitoes and other pests. (Always check to see if you are sensitive before using any product.)
3. **Invincible Herbal Insect Repellent from Great Garden Formulas by Joan Benjamin and Deborah L. Martin:** "...before heading outdoors, I douse myself with an incredible repellent that my friend Marion Spear and I concocted, Tina Wilcox, head gardener at the Ozark Folk Center in Mountain View, Arkansas says. "It renders me almost invincible to both insects and poison ivy!"

Ingredients and Supplies:

1 large handful fresh jewelweed *(Impatiens capensis)*
1 large glass jar with plastic lid (vinegar corrodes metal)
1 strainer
1 quart apple cider vinegar
½ teaspoon pennyroyal oil
1 teaspoon eucalyptus oil
1 teaspoon orange oil
1 teaspoon citronella oil
1 plastic spray bottle

Directions:

1. Crush jewelweed in the jar and cover with vinegar.
2. Let steep for several days.
3. Strain out the jewelweed and mix essential oils into the vinegar.
4. Before applying all over, spray a small amount on the inside of your arm and monitor for 15 minutes for any allergic reaction.
5. To use, spray thoroughly on clothing and lightly on any exposed skin except your face. Reapply every ½ hour or so. (To keep insects away from your face, spray your hat or bandanna.)

Yield: About 1 quart of invincible spray. Note: This formula will keep indefinitely. **Caution: If you are pregnant, don't use pennyroyal, even topically, as it may increase the risk of miscarriage. Note: Citronella oil has been known to attract female black bears.**

4. **Common Sense and Knowledge - Never approach bees during a thunderstorm. The electricity in the air makes them more aggressive.** There are over 700 species of venomous arthropods with those in the order Hymenoptera (ants, wasps, hornets and bees) accounting for the greatest

percentage of deaths, usually from an allergic reaction. Usually the only result is an unpleasant experience; even so, BEE CAREFUL! **If you feel an insect crawling on you, it should be brushed away and not crushed, slapped or pinched.** Remember to use mosquito netting, talcum powder, double-sided tape, duct tape (sticky side up), glueboards, Vaseline (petroleum jelly), screens, caulk and vacuums; the best control is to avoid and/or exclude them.

NOTE: Not Nice to Lice® and Not Nice to Fleas® shampoos and/or Safe Solutions, Inc. protease enzyme cleaners and Lice R Gone® Shampoo remove itching and irritations caused by poison ivy and/or insect bites and stings.

CAUTION: Remember, people may be allergic to numerous things, e.g., aspirin, zinc, thiamine chloride, milk and/or peanuts, so always treat a small area before using any product, herb, soap, cleaner or material on your body. When in doubt, always see your health care professional!

BE SURE TO 🕮READ THE APPROPRIATE SECTION IN <u>THE BEST CONTROL II</u>© FOR FURTHER COMMENTS, TREATMENTS AND/OR CONTROLS FOR SPECIFIC PESTS. BEE CAREFUL!

ALTERNATIVES YOU CAN USE TO SAFELY ELIMINATE COMMON PESTS IN AND AROUND HOMES, APARTMENTS, SCHOOLS AND WORKPLACES

In the following sections we have truly attempted to tell you some of the easiest, fastest, safest, most inexpensive and most effective practical ways to eliminate many of the most common pests in and around your home. We have only talked generically about pest control, e.g., roaches and not discussed in this small volume the many differences between German roaches or American roaches or any other individual species. We have attempted to list the most practical and simplest choices first. Some of these treatments may not be appropriate for children and pets, or even for you, so please use the safest alternative or leave the pest problem alone. We have only included controls for only some of the most common pests; even so, you should be able to safely control most pest problems in your home with the "tools" in this little book. For more details or information about other pest problems and hundreds of other alternative pest controls, read Steve Tvedten's book on CD-ROM entitled The Best Control© available at www.getipm.com or call 1-800-221-6188. For even greater details and thousands of safe and far more effective alternative pest controls, read The Best Control II© on CD-ROM.

The use of Intelligent Pest Management™ or IPM prevents or greatly decreases the number of pests and the potential pest damage. It costs less, is more effective and is far safer than the use of volatile pesticide poisons. The goal of true IPM approach should always be to manage pests and the environment so as to balance costs, benefits, human health and environmental quality. IPM programs apply a holistic approach to pest management emphasizing natural biological methods, and the appropriate use of selective, safer products called Pestisafes®.

Basic Knowledge: You must first find out what pests you have and then what they want and need. Why do they want to stay in and around your home? Eliminate these factors and, obviously, most indoor or outdoor pests will be eliminated in direct proportion to your efforts.

If you must use spot applications of non-volatile pesticide poisons, use them only as a last resort, but only after trying all other options first and, by law, use them only according to the labeled instructions.

PREVENTION - This is the Very Best Control or Defense. It is the beginning of Intelligent Pest Management®.

To an insect or rodent, your home or building and its surroundings is a macro-environment consisting of thousands of micro-environments; many with their own "climate", moisture, temperature, food and/or conditions conducive to their invasion or infestation. All creatures have the same four requirements we have for survival: food, water, shelter, and warmth. Most structure invading pests are controlled when you simply survival: food, water, shelter, and warmth. Most structure invading pests are controlled when you simply control water (moisture for drinking and the relative humidity) because water is their most critical survival factor. So properly ventilate, install and maintain dehumidifiers, fans and/or air conditioners and quickly correct/repair all moisture problems.

Inspection: The second best control you can use is to conduct a proper and thorough inspection - 90% of your pest problem will be in 10% of your building or lawn. If you don't see anything during the day, conduct a nighttime search and destroy mission using a red (or black) light. You must look everywhere.

Imagination and Common Sense: The third best control is your mind; it is 200,000 times bigger than most of your pests, so think before you act - many controls can be as simple as vacuuming up the pest, closing a window or vent, caulking, stepping on the "bug" or tuning on a fan or dehumidifier. **Common sense is not too common.**

Decrease moisture: Properly install and maintain vents, vapor barriers, fans, air conditioners, and/or dehumidifiers. Moisture is the major destructive factor to homes and the major key to pest control elimination. Control moisture and you control pests and damage to your building.

KEEPING THEM OUT

Exclusion: Seal cracks: The first defense is making sure pests don't get into your home. Crawling pests enter through cracks in or around the foundation or siding or doors and windows, while flying insects usually come in through open doors and windows. An annual inspection of the foundation and siding to caulk cracks (use good quality sealant) is a good idea. Be particularly careful to seal around exterior plumbing and electrical outlets. Make sure that door thresholds have good weather stripping under them and that the door and windows seal well when shut. Check that screens on windows, crawl space vents, and attic vents are intact and sealed around the edges. Remember 80% - 90% of all insect infestations migrate from the outside into your structure. Only 5 types of pests are generally carried inside buildings to create pest infestations; they are German cockroaches, fleas, stored product pests, mice and Pharaoh ants, so inspect for them. Don't forget to install door sweeps.

Use of screens: Window screens are excellent for keeping insects out of a house, but screen doors are not very effective. This is because flies and mosquitoes are attracted to people or food odors so they hang around outside screen doors and whisk inside every time the door is opened. Try to ventilate the house adequately without screen doors, at least on heavily used entrances. If screen doors are used, they should have strong spring closures that shut the door quickly and tightly.

Use of glueboards, duct tape and repellents: Prevent many pest invasions by properly using glueboards or duct tape and by sprinkling dry Tide laundry soap powder or talcum powder or medicated body powder or Comet® or food-grade DE as a barrier inside and outside.

Manage lights: Good design and management of exterior lighting is important to prevent insect problems.

- Avoid leaving porch lights on all evening to collect a cloud of moths and other insects and/or predators, e.g., bats. Every time the door is opened, the insects swirling around the light are swept into the house. Minimize the attraction time by turning porch lights on only when they are needed. Sensor lights that switch on in response to motion are ideal because they light the area for arriving guests, but switch off after a few minutes (saves energy too).

- When designing the lighting around the exterior of a new home, don't put light fixtures directly above the doors, especially over doors to decks or patios that might be used a lot in the evening. Place flood or spot lights a few feet away from the door and direct the light onto porches and stairs. This illuminates them safely, while keeping the mesmerized insects away from your door.
- Use yellow bulbs in yard light fixtures; flies and moths are not as attracted to yellow as they are to ordinary white light bulbs, or try sodium vapor lighting.

Manage the garbage: Keep garbage in sturdy, tightly covered containers and wash them out regularly with Safe Solutions, Inc. Enzyme Cleaner with Peppermint and borax. This prevents flies from breeding and reduces the attraction for ants, yellowjackets and other insects. If the kitchen food garbage can be composted daily, the trash will contain little that is attractive to insects. Where composting is not possible, tightly wrap up kitchen garbage, take it out frequently to a covered trash can, and dispose of it in sealed plastic bags. Avoid letting old clothes, newspapers, paper bags, cardboard, empty cans, and other trash accumulate in storage rooms, garages, etc., as these provide breeding sites for many household pests.

Manage your soil: Healthy, organic soil prevents many pest and weed problems.

Always remember: No one control will ever work in every situation. Try the simplest and safest control first and then, if that doesn't work, try some of the other control suggestions or a combination of the safer control suggestions. If you still don't get control, 🕮read the appropriate chapter in The Best Control© or The Best Control II©.

A FEW OF MY FAVORITE OFFENSIVE WEAPONS OR PEST CONTROL "TOOLS" OR PESTISAFES®!

If I asked you to roll around and/or climb on concertina (razor) barb wire - you would think the request absurd - yet ants can climb all over it without harm - you can powder your baby's bottom with talcum powder, but ants will leave an area where talcum is sprinkled.

Volatile, synthetic pesticide poisons were basically invented to kill man - why try using them on insects? Unlike the "professional" pest control industry that only has one "tool" to control pest problems -volatile, synthetic pesticide poisons - we want you to begin to understand my "tool box". The following are only a few of my favorite things or "tools" or Pestisafes® to control or repel the species of pesticide resistant insects that annoy man and/of that damage his crops and/or the other nuisance wildlife that "bug" him.

The poison "industry" and "some" regulating people want to "register" these Pestisafes® as "pesticides" because they kill, repel and/or control pests better than "their" *registered* economic pesticide poisons do - to them I ask the simple question, "If I crush a resistant ant with an ice cube and then the ice cube melts, is the moisture and/or vapor still an unregistered 'pesticide'?" It is my understanding that all materials generally recognized as safe (GRAS) and/or naturally occurring things do not need to be legally registered unless you want to claim or make them all proprietary products.

We know that if we try to kill a pest with "their" volatile, synthetic pesticide poisons - "their" poisons and *inerts* often can and do remain behind to contaminate and harm us, our children, pets, food, water, homes and environment for a long time - the toxic pesticide poisons that remain to contaminate and create pesticide resistance are not simply moisture or vapor, but dangerous poisons! It seems simply amazing and implausible to me that my techniques and Pestisafes® that are safer, less expensive, more effective, scientifically provable, field tested and result oriented would meet such resistance - especially from "open-minded scientists." But, to them, I would say you can not serve the public and your own selfish, archaic interests. **You either love your fellow man or you love money and power more**.

1. **BAITS - Why use baits?**

- Make the pests help do their own pest control by taking the toxin where it will kill the others
- No or low odor
- Little or no volatility
- Low % active ingredient
- Low volume application
- High % mortality
- Good service life
- Safety - less risk - Caution: Any time you make a toxic bait (even with borax or food-grade DE) add green food color to the bait and note on it clearly - **"Not for human consumption."**

Baiting for German cockroaches:

- Perform a thorough inspection. You will need a "red or yellow" flashlight at night.
- Put bait as close as you can to the cockroaches. Make it easy for them! Bait detection zone is about 12"; apply small amounts of bait in many places.
- Use enough bait to feed the entire cockroach population. For example: A baiting program wasn't "working", and the PCO still saw cockroaches. But when he checked, the PCO found the bait was all gone. He didn't use enough bait to feed/kill off all the population.
- Do a follow-up evaluation on any bait's performance - 10 - 14 days.

Caution: If you kill cockroaches and they die inside your building, you will breathe them in a few months.

Termite baits are just starting to be introduced and be used. The best termite bait station is the made of rolled cardboard and described in The Best Control II©. A termite bait station to be effective must be properly placed near the structure, but away from soils contaminated with termiticide poisons. Virtually any diluted antibiotic or salt spray will quickly kill a feeding colony of termites. As EPA and environmental concerns limit traditional termiticides, people will rely more on baits. Trying to get a feel for the colony is important for treatments, esp. baits. Worker termites and supplemental queens are the ones to key on with your bait treatments. Placement is important. Use ½% - 1% disodium octoborate tetrahydrate or table salt or borax as the maximum amount of toxin in your (cardboard or cellulose insulation) baits, or use Flagyl® or goldenseal which also helps to kill the protozoa and bacteria in their guts.

2. BENEFICIALS - Beneficial insects are classified into two major groups: 1) Predators that attack, kill, and eat their prey and 2) Parasites which lay eggs in or on a host which later hatch and kill the host. Pathogens are a third group of beneficial organisms e.g., bacteria, viruses, and/or fungi which invade the host and cause disease. Insects, nematodes, BT, milky spore, decollate snails, microbial fungicides, streptomycin bacteria, lacewings, predatory mites, lady bugs, praying mantis, earwigs, yellow jackets, and/or predator wasps, mealy bug destroyers, etc. The costs are varied and the types of beneficials extremely varied, e.g., the lacewing is not mobile at the time of application and must be applied directly to the infested area, while adult lady bugs can be released to find their own target pests, but lady bugs are captured and not raised and may be out of stock. There are many suppliers and, as with most trends, you can expect more to come on line. Many of the companies who supply beneficials also employ consultants. These consultants typically have a wealth of knowledge regarding specific traits and tendencies that each beneficial is capable of demonstrating. The 5 listed below are just a fraction of what is out there:

IPM LABORATORIES
Main Street
Locke, NY 13092-0300
1-315-497-3129
www.ipmlabs.com

ARBICO Environmental
P. O. Box 4247CRB
Tucson, AZ 85738
1-800-827-2847 (BUGS)
www.arbico.com

Kunafin
Rte. 1 - Box 39
Quemado, TX 7877
1-800-832-1113
www.kunafin.com

Rincon-Vitova Insectaries, Inc.
P. O. Box 1555
Ventura, CA 93002-1555
1-800-248-2847 (BUGS)
www.rinconvitova.com

Biocontrol Network
5116 Williamsburg Rd.
Brentwood, TN 37027
1-800-441-2847 (BUGS)
www.usit.net/BICONET

Biological control of pests involves the use of one living organism to control another. For example, most arthropod pests have natural enemies or disease organisms that control or suppress them effectively under some conditions or in some situations. Occasionally insects or microorganisms contribute to the control of certain weeds. Many microorganisms also provide natural control of pest birds and rodents. Sometimes biological control can be an important component of a pest management program by taking advantage of these helpful organisms. **When natural enemies or microorganisms are present, efforts can be made to protect them so they may increase in number and help control pests more effectively.**

One of the first references to natural pest control comes from J. C. London (1850) in his "Encyclopedia of Gardening (Book III, pg. 819) when he suggested a toad kept in a mushroom house will eat worms, ants and other insects, but to most people the idea would be disgusting of a toad crawling over anything intended for the table."

3. BORAX, OR SODIUM TETRABORATE, - is a combination of sodium, boron and oxygen, and is mined from the soil in its crude form. Boric acid is a crystalline material derived from borax. Caution: Remember, boric acid and all boron products can act as a stomach poison when ingested. While 20 Mule Team Borax® is extremely effective in controlling or eliminating ants, termites, weeds, lice, fleas, spiders and roaches, the Dial Corporation notes, "This product has not been tested nor received approval from the EPA for use as a pesticide." Even so if you mop or spray the floors, voids, sill boxes, tunnels, backs of furniture, appliances and other areas where you see insect pests with borax - you will be surprised on how great the material controls virtually all pests. It has been used for years to make cellulose insulation insect free and fire retardant. It also is great for removing stains in carpeting and/or odors in urinals, etc. - so mop to remove odors and to help clean - in doing so you will also control pests "accidentally". In their 1920 - 1928 Burroughs Welcome & Co. (USA) Inc. catalogue they note borax *(Sodii boras)* is an antiseptic, used for lotions, mouthwashes, and gargles. Also given internally for epilepsy. Note: Chroma Trim Gum® includes 200 mcg of boron (as sodium borate) as a "food supplement". The use of borax to disinfect: Mix ½ cup of borax in 1 gallon of hot water to disinfect all surfaces. This mix will also inhibit mold growth. **Borax and boron products should not be eaten or ingested! Be careful not to contaminate food, utensils, pets or people.**

4. BORIC ACID - Boric acid and its salts have been used for pest control for over a hundred years, and in folk remedies for more than 1000 years. Boric acid baits have been used since the late 1800's. Boric acid has been used in medicine since the time of Lister in the 1860's. It was first used to protect wood in the U. S. in the 1920's against blue stain fungi. The fire retardant properties of boric acid were discovered in the 1930's. Celcure® was patented in 1933 to prevent wood fungi decay. These substances are various forms of boron which also routinely is found normally circulating at low levels in our blood streams. Boric acid and other insecticidal dusts are inorganic pesticides that have other uses besides their insect killing power. For example, boric acid is a wonderful pesticide as a 99.95% pure dust formulation, but in a 1% water solution, it is commonly used as an eyewash. Most dust formulations have an abrasive action on the insect which removes the waxy coating on the exterior of the insect's body. The waxy coating is used to retain water and without it the insect quickly dies from dehydration. **Be careful not to contaminate food, utensils, pets or people with any (boron) product!**

5. BUG JUICE COCKTAIL - Blend ½ cup aphids or 1 cup infested leaves and 2 cups water strain and spray. If you see a handful or two of your garden's cabbage loopers are chalky white and weak - they are infected with nuclear polyhedrosis virus (NPV) - put loopers in blender with water, strain and spray over crops. The remaining pests will die in several days - try a mixture of bugs, strain, and spray. Collect ½ cup of any specific pest and mash well. Mix with 2 cups water, and strain. Mix ¼ cup of this bug juice and a few drops of soap with 2 cups of water, and spray. Don't make yourself sick, too! Use nonfood utensils, a mask and wear plastic gloves.

6. CARBON DIOXIDE FIRE EXTINGUISHERS OR DRY ICE - can be used to freeze pests, e.g., an entire hornet or wasp nest, which can then be safely removed and placed inside double plastic bags, frozen for several days or buried. You can also freeze other insects, e.g., roaches. **Carbon dioxide fumigation** has been widely used to treat stored grain. Grain bins and other structures have also been routinely treated with carbon dioxide to eradicate insect infestations. We believe the insect opens up its breathing apparati when exposed to high levels of CO_2 and then suffocates from the lack of oxygen. Carbon dioxide will also suffocate rats and other mammals in their tunnels. Concerns have been raised regarding the production of carbonic acid from the CO_2 and the water in the chamber and its subsequent danger.

7. CAULK - Seal all visible cracks, crevices, voids, and other openings (that you can insert a business card into) to prevent and/or control many pest problems.

8. CHARCOAL - Activated charcoal filters can remove dust mite and cockroach allergens and/or odors and clean chemicals out of the air when you put one on both sides of a running box window fan.

9. CHAROCAL BRIQUETTES - Lit briquettes create carbon monoxide and when placed in tunnels - carbon monoxide is heavier than air - and all living things die that breathe this gas. Be careful if you try this control and first check regarding any ordinances that would prohibit it's use.

10. DEHUMIDIFIERS - When properly installed, dehumidifiers (and/or air conditioners) reduce moisture and many pest problems including termites, mold, carpenter ants, mildew, roaches, sow bugs, earwigs, fungus, etc. are all eliminated or at a minimum greatly controlled. Air conditioners, fans, and/or dryers also help reduce the relative humidity - most insects/spiders/termites/fungus/mold/etc. need high levels of humidity to survive - often if you just reduce the humidity - you can control all of these pests. **Add a fan to increase the desiccant action.**

11. DETERGENTS - are surfactants, or surface active agents, basically washing compounds that mix with grease and water; they form a "bridge" between lipophilic substances and water-soluble substances and thus enhance penetration of water, insecticides, oils, or enzymes. Richards and Korda (1948) found that detergents disrupt not only the lipoid layer of the epicuticle but also the protein layers of the endocuticle. The properties rendering a detergent most effective are (1) enough liposolubility to penetrate and emulsify the epicuticular wax, (2) sufficient solubility in water (i.e., not excessively lipophilic), and (3) ability to penetrate the outer cement layer of the epicuticle. Obviously, once the cuticle is comprised by the detergents - insecticide poisons are not necessary to control the insects. Make sure your detergent does not have any hazardous or prohibited "inerts". While detergents are synthetic, some of their ingredients can be natural. Detergents were developed during World War II when the oils needed to make soap became scarce.

12. DIATOMACEOUS EARTH (DE) - Diatomaceous earth is a mineral product mined from the fossilized silica shell remains of unicellular or colonized algae from the class Bacillariaphyceae, better known as diatoms. There are many different companies that sell DE. The Author recommends the product sold by Safe Solutions, Inc. Most registered DE has pyrethrin and pipernoyl butoxide (PBO). Some unregistered (without pyrethrin and PBO) food-grade diatomaceous earth (DE) is safe enough to be eaten, yet will kill most crawling insects. Be sure you have the best quality. Make sure the DE you use meets World Health Organization (WHO) safety standards. WHO cautions that DE with a crystalline silica content over three percent (3%) is dangerous for ingestion by humans or animals. Safe Solutions, Inc. DE has less than 1% free silica. Swimming pool DE ranges from 60% to 70% free silica. **The Author does not recommend the use of swimming pool DE.** Safe Solutions, Inc. food-grade DE can be used as a dry dust or wettable powder. To make a wettable powder mix, use 4 tablespoons of product per gallon of water and add a ¼ teaspoon of Safe Solutions, Inc. Enzyme Cleaner per gallon of mix.

DiaFil (Fresh Water Diatoms)
(Scanning electron photomicrograph, X 1000)

The Safe Solutions, Inc. diatomaceous earth pictured above shows a well preserved, impurity-free DE product.

13. DUSTS - Road dust, talcum powder, Comet® cleanser and many other fine dusts kill insects by desiccation and/or suffocation. Dusts clog the spiracles or breathing holes of insects.

14. ENZYME CLEANERS - The 5th Edition of Truman's Scientific Guide to Pest Control Operations described "The Ideal Pesticide". "Ideally any pesticide will act rapidly on pests, yet be completely harmless to people, domestic animals, wildlife, and other aspects of the environment. Its residues would only last as long as was necessary to create the desired effect, usually for very short periods. It would also be inexpensive and readily available in necessary quantities, chemically stable (before application), non-flammable, and otherwise safe to use around homes or industrial sites. It would be easily prepared and applied, non-corrosive and non-staining, and it would have no undesirable odor. Unfortunately, no such (synthetic) pesticide exists."

Purdue University and Advanstar Communications (Pest Control Magazine) worked on this 1997 Pest Control Manual, but they were, obviously, still unaware the Author, Stephen L. Tvedten, had begun working with and using and field testing the perfect (pesticide) or Pestisafe™ based on natural pest control.

In addition to their (perfect pesticide poison descriptive) list, Safe Solutions, Inc. Enzyme Cleaner with (or without) Peppermint is, in the Author's opinion, the finest enzyme cleaner out there and it will never create any pest resistance problems, for it truly is the perfect pesticide and the entire compound contains only ingredients that are considered food grade or GRAS (Generally Recognized as Safe) and can be used virtually everywhere, even when people are sick, under 1, over 60, pregnant and/or chemically sensitive to control even pesticide-resistant pests.

The Author has watched insects and spiders die in 10 - 30 seconds when this particular enzyme cleaner is mixed at a rate of 1 oz. per quart of water. The U. S. EPA prohibits any/all claims that any registered pesticide poison is either safe or non-toxic. That is just another reason why the Author calls the Safe Solutions, Inc. Enzyme Cleaner with Peppermint a Pestisafe™ rather than a pesticide poison.

Insectivore plants produce and also use protease enzymes to digest their insect prey. Spiders produce and inject protease enzymes to predigest their prey and all molting insects produce a small amount of protease enzyme to serve as a chemical "zipper" so they can split open their exoskeletons when they molt and increase in their size; without the protease enzyme they would be trapped inside their own exoskeletons and be crushed to death by their own growth.

Fogging and/or lightly spraying Safe Solutions Enzyme Cleaner with Peppermint in or on gardens, lawns, orchards, fields, swamps, and/or directly on insects, washing floors, linen, clothing, pets, hair, etc. will quickly and safely result in virtually instant pest control. We strongly recommend you only use diluted Safe Solutions, Inc. Enzyme Cleaner with Peppermint (that contain protease enzymes) to control virtually all mites, arachnids, insects, fungus, mildew and mold pests. Most enzyme products or cleaners available at swimming pool supply or cleaning or janitorial supply houses use bacteria to create "their" enzymes, e.g., pet mess cleaners, drain openers and septic tank cleaners - some of the bacteria or acidic pH may be harmful to you and yours and none of them are patented or tested for this use. Use the U. S. patent pending and Australia patented Safe Solutions, Inc. Enzyme Cleaner with Peppermint at a rate of 1 oz. per quart of water to clean virtually everything and incidentally to control virtually all indoor pests or 1 - 2 oz. per head for lice control, or 1 oz. - 2 oz. per dog for flea control, or 1 oz. - 2 oz. per 3 gallons of water as a soak for ant nests, or 1 oz. per 4 gallons of water for agriculture use, or 1 oz. per gallon of water or for use as a floor cleaner.

The body surface of insects consists of a hard skin known as the cuticle - the major pesticide pathway is cuticular penetration. The insect cuticle is hydrophobic so that it can resist desiccation and drowning but the Safe Solutions, Inc. enzymes and surfactants quickly and safely cut through this protective shell. Synthetic pesticide poisons use light oils, dusts and/or volatile solvents to help penetrate this same cuticle. Caution: Remember, these Safe Solutions enzymes will kill all insects including beneficials - so use them outside with great discretion! Note: You can adjust the Safe Solutions, Inc. Enzyme Cleaner dilution rate (1 - 500 or about ¼ oz. of enzyme cleaner per gallon of water) when spraying to control soft-bodied pests, e.g., aphids - lady bugs and other beneficials will not be destroyed at this rate. Gabriel Cousins, M.D. has stated, "All life depends on enzyme function. When our enzymes are deplete, so is our vital force and health." **Be careful to spray a few leaves and check if any plant is sensitive before you spray the entire plant. You should also spray a small area first to see if there is any sensitivity or staining before washing to spraying the entire animal, plant or area.** You can purchase Safe Solutions, Inc. Enzyme Cleaner with (or without) Peppermint by calling the office at 1-888-443-8738 or from its web site at: http://www.safesolutionsinc.com. This cleaner is not sold by Safe Solutions, Inc. as a pesticide.

15. EXCLUSION - Keep pests from entering with screens, properly fitting doors and windows, caulk, cement, rodent guards, etc. You can fill large voids/cavities with aerosol foam insulation. **Screening Caution**: rodent guards, etc. You can fill large voids/cavities with aerosol foam insulation. **Screening Caution**: Screening will severely restrict air flow into vents, so if you need to screen vents, build a box with a surface area large enough to allow proper air flow. Your screen manufacturer will provide you with tables that determine how much the air flow will be restricted.

16. FANS - will control roaches in kitchens if left on 24 hours a day for several weeks and when used outside will safely keep mosquitoes at bay. To control dust and dust mites take a (square box) window fan, using duct tape attach two furnace filters (cut to size) to the fan grills on both the intake and exhaust sides. Turn on the fan and it will filter dust and mites from the air - use activated charcoal filters and you also remove odors, pesticides and increase filtration results. **Change charcoal filters as needed.**

17. HAIR DRYERS - can be used to control fungus and roaches and other pests - simply direct the hot, dry air at them or where they hide and see what happens next.

18. IMAGINATION - this is the greatest pest control "tool" ever - some people have no imagination and are doomed to only use more and more "registered" poison to "control" less and less their pests. Look around, think, ask and develop new tools all of the time. Imagination combined with intelligence can not be beaten. Imagination is more important than knowledge. Knowledge is very restrictive; imagination is unlimited. **Your brain is 200,000 times bigger than that of the insect pest, so use it and you will win; use volatile, "registered" pesticide poisons and you will lose!**

19. INSECT REPELLENTS - You can make an effective insect repellent using 75% coconut oil, 15% water, 4% soybean oil, 3% geranium oil and 3% vanilla. You can also lightly rub Vicks VapoRub®, Noxema®, cedar oil, lavender oil, pennyroyal oil, sweet basil, peppermint oil, citronella oil, eucalyptus oil or scented geraniums on your body and clothes. Dilute all fragrant oils in coconut oil, vegetable oil or almond oil first. A strong infusion of chamomile tea can be applied to the skin or fur to repel insects. Baby powder with talcum will repel many crawling insects. **Always test a small area of your skin** (with a small amount) to see if you get a reaction before treating the entire area or body.

20. LIGHTS - Can be used to inspect or repel or attract pests. Red light as the only light source allows you to check for roaches and carpenter ants at night. Black light makes rodent urine and scorpions fluoresce. Yellow light (bug lights) and sodium vapor lighting will not attract as many insects. Regular (white) or black light can attract insects to your trap or vacuum.

21. PETROLEUM JELLY - Many insects are attracted to yellow, white, or blue colors - use an index card as a trap by covering it with sticky petroleum jelly, STP® or honey - most insects, e.g., earwigs are repelled by petroleum jelly - so you can use sticky petroleum jelly to make your roach traps escape proof. Most insects will not cross over petroleum jelly barriers, so use them to "fence out" pests.

22. PLAIN WATER - a strong stream is effective in destroying aphids, mealy bugs, mud dauber nests, and red spider mites. It also makes cats and dogs leave your yard quickly.

23. SALT - Salt sprinkled on weeds that sprout in paved areas, along fence lines, driveways or wherever you want - salt will kill all plants including "weeds"; salt or salt water sprays will also kill snails and slugs. Salt will kill fleas and lice on people or animals and termites and numerous other pests. CAUTION: It will damage plants and will not remove nits. Many salts can be used to pretreat soil and wood for termite control, but some salts will also destroy ferrous metals, e.g., nails.

24. SOAP - Soaps are also surfactants, but they are made with natural ingredients; they may be used as alternatives to control insects, algae, moss and weeds. Mix 4 ounces of virtually any soap - mild (unregistered) dish soap or a natural soap or a commercial cleaner or a degreaser in 1 gallon of water and spray as an insecticide to quickly control most insect pests or use an (registered) insecticidal or herbicidal soap, e.g., Safers® or Ringer®. Be sure your cleaner does not contain alkylphenol polyethoxylate - which is a hormone disrupter. Spray floors and yards to control ants and fleas. This mix will also control many insects, e.g., white flies, mites, aphids, etc. Spray a few leaves and wait 48 hours if there is no ill effect - spray your plants every 2 - 3 days for several weeks. **Caution: Some plants and beneficial insects are very sensitive to small amounts of soap.** Use 1 tablespoon of dish soap and 1 teaspoon of vegetable oil for each quart of water and spray to control aphids, spider mites, scales, some caterpillars and mealy bugs - this "brew" is effective against eggs as well as adults. **If it is sunny and/or the temperature is over 85°F. the oil may damage some foliage.** Deodorant soaps especially Dial® can repel deer and other animals. Sprinkle dry soap into garbage cans after they have been washed and allowed to dry; it acts as a fly repellent. Sprinkle or spray Tide laundry soap around the foundation of your home to keep ants out. At 40o F. or less spraying birds with soapy water will quickly kill them. The "original" Pestisafe®. **Soap and water** - When Grandmother finished washing the dishes she threw the soapy water on her plants and flowers controlling most insect pests quickly and safely.

25. SPRAY BOTTLE CURES - Non-toxic "pesticide" sprays that can be made from ingredients readily available in the home. We prefer to call them Pestisafes®.

a. **All-purpose** - Take an empty spray bottle and fill about ¾ of the way with water, then add a few drops of Ivory liquid soap, some hot peppers or hot pepper sauce and some garlic. This works well, but needs to be reapplied after every storm and/or every couple of weeks.
b. **All-purpose** - Grind together three hot peppers, three large onions, and at least one whole clove of garlic. Cover mash with water and place in a covered container. Let container stand over night. Strain mixture through cheesecloth or a fine strainer and add enough water to make a gallon of spray.
c. **All-purpose** - Mix one tablespoon of a mild dish washing detergent plus one teaspoon of a vegetable cooking oil with one quart of water. This can be sprayed on all plants. Remember to spray both the top and the underside of the leaves. You can also add 1 teaspoon (rounded) of baking soda if you have fungus problems.
d. **All-purpose** - Finely chop 10 to 15 garlic cloves and soak in 1 pint of mineral oil for 24 hours. Strain and add enough water to make a gallon of spray. Test on a few leaves to see if the plant is damaged and spray as is, or add a few drops of soap for extra stickiness.
e. **All-purpose** - Blend ½ cup of hot peppers with 2 cups of water. Strain and spray.
f. **All-purpose** - Combine 1 to 2 cups of rubbing alcohol with 1 quart of water. Test spray and let stand overnight to see if damage occurs to plant.
g. Orange trees and rosebushes - **Soak macerated tomato, rhubarb or oleander leaves in water** and apply as spray onto leaves and branches. **Be careful; these leaves are very toxic.**
h. **Red spider mites, spiders, cabbage worms, and weeds** - An ounce of table salt to a gallon of water has been shown to stop these pests. Use a tablespoon of salt to two gallons of water for the worms. Be careful - salt damages plants! Straight salt, especially in non-garden areas can stop weeds and termites in protected areas, e.g., crawl spaces, but can kill plants and harm ferrous metals.
i. **Species specific** - Collect ½ cup of a specific pest and mash well or blend. Mix this with two cups of water and strain. Mix ¼ cup of this "bug juice" with 2 cups of water and a few drops of soap and spray.

Be sure you are not sensitive to any control suggestion and keep all controls out of the reach of children, pets and wildlife.

Caution: Some sprays can damage, discolor, kill or scorch foliage or irritate people or pets - always test a small, inconspicuous area first before treating the entire area, pet or person!

26. STEAMERS - Steamers are just entering the marketplace. The Author has used the Vapor Dragon to control pests and bacteria with steam.

27. SURFACTANTS - Are slightly viscous, clear amber substances or colloids that work as ("magnetic") cleaners and degreasers. Surfactants can be used as household, industrial and marine cleaners, personal hygiene products, insect repellents and pest (and bird) control compounds. A micelle is a colloid, microscopic particle formed by an aggregation of small biodegradable molecules. Each molecule has a hydrophilic (water-seeking) pole and a hydrophobic (water-repelling) pole. The hydrophobic poles attract each other, forming the interior of the micelle and the hydrophilic poles form the outer surface. When a single micelle or surfactant molecule comes in contact with a hydrocarbon molecule (grease, oil, wax, binders, etc.), the hydrophobic center of the micelle or surfactant quickly bonds via homologous attraction to the hydrophobic hydrocarbon site, locking it into a colloidal suspension, pulling the hydrocarbon into the micelle and lifting the hydrophobic hydrocarbon molecule from its original surface. This emulsification process easily penetrates highly viscous, dirty and/or sticky materials, lifting them off.

Unregistered surfactants are routinely added to or used in pesticide poison formulations, but we have found they often work better alone. If sprayed all alone, some "regulators" then call these same surfactants "unregistered pesticides". Because the exoskeletal structures, wax and joints of insects are basically all comprised of hydrocarbon molecules, insects, gnats, mosquitoes, flies, etc. may avoid surfaces upon which diluted of hydrocarbon molecules, insects, gnats, mosquitoes, flies, etc. may avoid surfaces upon which diluted surfactants or (colloidal) micelles have been sprayed for two days or more. When sprayed directly with surfactants, (which cause the micellation) insects, mites, mold, bacteria, etc. will all die quickly because of the lifting of hydrocarbon molecules (they literally are dismantled)!

Surfactants are considered to be biodegradable and basically innocuous to people and pets, but will often kill fleas, lice, ticks and other pests while washing or upon contact. If ingested, they may cause diarrhea primarily due to the emulsification of grease and oil in the digestive tract. The surfactants in Safe Solutions, Inc. Enzyme Cleaner with Peppermint are basically the same as those found in a dish detergent.

28. TALCUM POWDER AND/OR MEDICATED BODY POWDERS - Control and/or repel many pests when sprinkled around. Some people consider talcum powder to be carcinogenic and/or dangerous - but, given the opportunity to choose using a little talcum powder that actually stops most ants immediately or using some volatile poison that does not work as well - I would choose talcum powder - my answer is very simple when you consider the question in reverse would you prefer to dust a baby's bottom with talcum powder or a "registered" poison? Actually there are grades of talcum powder - some contain asbestos and are not safe - as far as I know baby powder does not contain asbestos. Talcum powder quickly dries out the insect and/or clogs the spiracles and, thereby, kills many insects. Talc (non-asbestis form) does typically contain crystalline silica at levels greater than 0.1% but less than 1.0%. Silica has been determined to be a Class 2A carcinogen by IARC. Repeated exposures can cause talcosis, a pulmonary fibrosis, which may lead to severe and permanent lung damage, possibly leading to disability and death, so use it with care. I would also mention that talc is an ingredient in Tums Antacid/Calcium supplement. Talcum powder will repel/control fire ants and other insect pests and nuisance wildlife. Try to use corn starch as a replacement in vacuums to suffocate vacuumed pests; **always pick the safest alternative**.

29. TEMPERATURE - Increase or lower temperatures even 30_{o} to 40_{o} and you safely and quickly control many insect pests - change the temperature even more drastically and/or quickly and you can control virtually all pests. Unlike mammals, many cold-blooded organisms (insects included) are at the mercy of quickly changing temperature extremes. If climatic temperature increases occur over a developmental period of months or years - a given insect may gradually acquire the ability to survive, this is termed "acclimatization". If an insect can overcome gradual temperature stresses in days, hours, or even minutes this short-term adjustment is called "acclimation". **Most insects quickly die if you quickly change their temperature.**

30. VACUUMS - Vacuums quickly remove insects, spiders, food, debris, eggs, body parts, etc. - if you are vacuuming up live insects or pests be sure to put a little talcum powder or corn starch in your bag first to suffocate the pests - use a HEPA filter and a red light at night to get nocturnal pests, e.g., roaches. Use a dusting brush to vacuum up spider mites on the underside of leaves or whiteflies both from the air and on household plants. If you use a rinse-and-vac, be sure to include some soapy water to drown the pests.

31. VENTILATION - Moisture reduction by proper (basement, crawl and attic) ventilation, fans and/or dehumidifiers, plumbing and rain gutter repairs, roofing etc. is a primary factor in controlling most structural insects and fungal problems. Excessive moisture attracts or creates conditions favorable to many insect, fungus and mold problems.

32. VINEGAR - Spray weeds and pest plants with vinegar. White vinegar will also kill ants. Vinegar attracts wasps, fungus gnats and fruit flies - put 2" in a long necked bottle - add a few drops of liquid soap or enzyme cleaner - and they will crawl in and won't be able to crawl out. To deodorize concrete, scrub with Safe Solutions, Inc. Enzyme Cleaner with (or without) Peppermint or a solution of half white vinegar and water or undiluted denatured alcohol as needed. Vinegar is an acid that can be used to soothe the alkaline sting of a wasp. Mix 3 parts vinegar (10% acidity) with 1 part dishwashing soap and spray weeds to kill them. White vinegar sprays repel cats and small dishes of white vinegar absorb odors.

33. THE USE OF VINEGAR AND HYDROGEN PEROXIDE TO DISINFECT - Now, you can safely disinfect your home and food - without exposing your family to toxic synthetic chemicals. You can make your own inexpensive sprays that actually work better disinfecting than any commercial synthetic disinfectant. All you have to purchase from the drug store is some (fresh) three percent hydrogen peroxide and some plain white or apple cider vinegar from the grocery store. Put them full strength in their own clean spray bottles.

If you want to safely disinfect vegetables or fruit, just spray or thoroughly mist them with the vinegar and then the hydrogen peroxide (or the hydrogen peroxide and then the vinegar), and then rinse them off under running water. Using first one spray and then the other, you can also safely and effectively disinfect food preparation surfaces and other washable surfaces and materials. You won't cause stains on most surfaces, nor will you have any lingering taste of vinegar or hydrogen peroxide on your food, and you will not harm you or your family or the environment.

From Our Toxic Times, May 2001: Heinz Company spokesperson Michael Mullen references numerous studies to show that a straight 5% solution of vinegar—such as you buy in the supermarket—kills 99% of bacteria, 82% of mold and 80% of germs (viruses). He noted that Heinz can't claim on its packaging that vinegar is a disinfectant since the Company has not registered it as a pesticide with the Environmental Protection Agency (EPA).

In tests run at Virginia Polytechnic Institute and State University, pairing the two mists killed virtually all *Salmonella, Shigella,* or *E.coli* bacteria on heavily contaminated food and surfaces when used in this fashion, making this spray combination more effective at killing these potentially lethal bacteria than chlorine bleach or any commercially available kitchen cleaner.

The best results came from using one mist right after the other - it is 10 times more effective than using either spray by itself and more effective than mixing the vinegar and hydrogen peroxide in one sprayer.

ANT OVERVIEW

Ants are the most dominant group of social insects. In the savanna of the African Ivory Coast the density of ants is more than 7,000 colonies and 20 million individuals per hectare. Ants belong to the insect Order Hymenoptera and are close relatives of bees and wasps. Throughout the world there are over 20,000 species of ants, but only about 50 are known to be pests of the food or structures of man. Except for the polar regions and a couple of islands, they flourish on all land areas of the earth, from rain forests to deserts. All pest control technicians become involved with ant problems at some point in their career— most commonly because ants are found foraging or nesting inside structures - or because swarming ant reproductives are confused with swarming termites. Only a comparatively small proportion of ants cause damage - only these ants are considered to be pests around our homes and buildings because they feed on and contaminate our food stuffs, damage our wood structures, build unsightly mounds in our lawns and even fewer ants are aggressive and are able to inflict painful bites or stings. Most ants are extremely beneficial cleaning up mess after mess and up to 95% of all weed seeds! (They truly are nature's little garbage collecting ladies.)

Foraging - Ants are omnivores and eat a wide variety of food, including other insects, seeds, nectar, meats, greases, sugars and honeydew. Honeydew is a liquid produced by plant-sucking insects, such as aphids or plant, mealy bugs (groups of small insects with a white powder clinging to them), scale insects, and plant hoppers. These insects feed in groups on plant stems and leaves. Many species of ants protect these aggregations from other insects. Ants are a part of this pattern; they also take drops of honeydew continuously produced by the small sap-sucking individuals. Some ant species appear to just wander randomly; others trail each other precisely from colony to food and/or water source and back. Most ants follow structural guidelines as they travel, rather than in a straight "beeline". Ants communicate with each other using different methods, including pheromones, touch and stridulation (sound production), for transmitting messages. Workers foraging for food attract attention and communicate their messages when they return to the colony. Honey seems to really attract honeydew-eating ants. Add 5% or less boric acid or sodium borate or food-grade DE to make an excellent sweet bait which has both a food attractant and a convenient moisture source.

ANT CONTROL AND MANAGEMENT - The best control for ants is cleanliness. The ant's greatest enemies are other ants. It is important to note that all of the ants found indoors, only a few species are responsible for the majority of infestations; some species are not common inside a structure but appear sporadically; and other types of ants are found inside only under rare or accidental conditions. While the third group is difficult to prepare for, the first group will be studied, discussed, and control experiences analyzed. The middle group may take an inordinate amount of your time, with inconclusive results. These elusive ants may appear several times in one year, then not be encountered for several years. Some are more or less common in some regions and uncommon in others. Remember, most ant infestations originate outside the building.

I have found schools that have been sprayed with various volatile, synthetic pesticide poisons once a week for 15 years or more without every getting "control". Ants are the most common cause of callbacks for the pest control industry, so why use their volatile poisons?

Inspection - The key to virtually any ant control is to find the nest. All ants are social insects that live cooperatively in a colony. Large numbers of ants can be killed without ever solving your pest infestation. Keep a daily log or record of where ants are seen. Bait the workers with jelly, peanut butter, cut-up crickets, oils, proteins, etc., and follow them back to their nests, or inspect with a yellow or red light at night.

Habitat Alteration

- Sprinkling food-grade diatomaceous earth, Comet® or Tide® laundry powder/soap or planting mint and lavender or lightly spraying Safe Solutions, Inc. Enzyme Cleaner with Peppermint around the building or dog runs are a delightful deterrents/repellants.
- Caulk all wall penetrations and mortar masonry cracks. Wall penetrations include utility lines, air conditioning, refrigerant pipes, phone lines, etc.
- Tighten all door and window frames. Sprinkle food-grade DE, talcum powder, baking soda, Comet® and/ or medicated body powders where the ants are entering.
- Repair water leaks. (Remember, carpenter ants love to nest in insulation, especially if it is damp.)
- Trim all shrubbery and branches away from house. Remove mulch.
- Remove any firewood that is stacked close to buildings; boards, stones, etc. that encourage nesting; screen openings in hollow pillars, columns, and ventilators.
- Control ant-tended aphids and mealybugs Safe Solutions, Inc. Enzyme Cleaner with (or without) Peppermint diluted ¼ oz. per gallon.

Intelligent Pest Management®

- **Conduct a thorough inspection**. Spray and/or mop with borax. (Use ½ cup of borax per gallon of hot water. Remember to keep borax away from plants, surfaces/areas that food, children or pets touch.)
- **Consider the species when choosing bait**. Some excellent all purpose bait choices include Light Karo Syrup, cornstarch, honey, molasses, peanut butter and/or jelly. Use baits with non-volatile stomach poisons, e.g., boric acid, borax or sodium borate. Baits are excellent in critical areas, e.g., computer or hospital rooms. Mix (5% or less) food-grade DE, boric acid (or borax) into any food you see the ants eating - if the ants die by the poisoned bait - use less boric acid or borax - **be careful not to allow children, pets or wildlife to eat these toxic baits.** Remember to routinely switch from carbohydrate back to protein baits, or use both. Do not spray or dust

around baits. Never store baits or bait materials where they can be contaminated with any other odors, especially smoke or fumes of volatile pesticides. Ants and other insects can detect minute amounts of foreign or repellent chemicals and will avoid chalk lines, calcium chloride, baking soda, food-grade DE, Comet®, talcum powder and other dusts.

Fire Ant Repellent: Lightly sprinkle baby powder with talc or food-grade DE on shoes, socks, cuffs and legs to protect yourself.

INTELLIGENT CONTROLS FOR ANTS

1. **Be sure to trim all branches** that touch or overhang the building and caulk all visible cracks, crevices and other openings. Make ant barriers with petroleum jelly, Comet®, talcum powder, food-grade DE or medicated powder. Maintain routine and thorough sanitation. **Caulk all openings to the exterior and install door sweeps.**
2. **Routinely clean** with Safe Solutions, Inc. Enzyme Cleaner with Peppermint (1 oz. per gallon) and/or borax (½ cup per gallon of hot water), empty garbage and vacuum daily. Carefully caulk/seal all cracks and crevices where a nest is suspected. Properly store food and garbage. Vacuum up all visible ants.
3. **Lightly sprinkle** food-grade DE, talcum powder, baking soda, Tide® soap or freshly ground pepper or calcium chloride (Comet®) outside and lightly dust with talcum or Comet® or calcium chloride dust or baking soda or medicated body powder or food-grade DE inside along the edges and in all remaining cracks, crevices and sill-boxes. Keep food and garbage properly stored away from ants. Improve drainage. Trim all branches that touch or overhang the building. Put bands of Tanglefoot ® or STP® oil treatment or petroleum jelly around the perimeter of infested trees.
4. **Mix 45% baking soda and 45% powdered sugar and 10% dry active yeast or powdered vitamin C** and place the bait mix wherever you see ants. Mix 5% - 10% food-grade DE in honey or (fermenting type) molasses. The only way to eliminate ants permanently is to destroy the queen(s).
5. **Spray ant trails** with diluted Safe Solutions, Inc. Enzyme Cleaner with Peppermint or Lemon Joy® or vinegar or perfume or sprinkle talc or food-grade DE or freshly ground pepper or calcium chloride (Comet®) or baking soda, or draw a line of chalk or petroleum jelly where you do not want them to cross. Properly install and maintain dehumidifiers. Eliminate moisture problems and improve ventilation.

6. **Spray all visible ants** with diluted Safe Solutions, Inc. Enzyme Cleaner with Peppermint (1 oz. per quart of water) or vacuum them up.
7. **Spray nests** with white vinegar, Safe Solutions, Inc. Enzyme Cleaner with Peppermint or Fantastic®, or sprinkle them with talcum (baby) powder, calcium chloride dust, medicated body powder, food-grade DE, Comet® or crushed chalk. Fumigate with carbon dioxide or steam them. **Finding and then eliminating the nest is the most effective ant control technique.**
8. **Make your own fresh borax or boric acid baits** using their preferred foods, e.g., a liquid bait can be made with ½ teaspoon (or less) of boric acid in 2½ fluid oz. of honey or corn syrup or molasses - heat and stir until the boric acid or borax is dissolved completely - mix in at least 1 - 2 equal parts of water (dilute the bait more if you see dead ants by the bait) then put in small vials or lids or small tin foil "cups" where you have seen ant activity - **but safely out of the reach of children, pets and wildlife**. Bait until control is achieved (usually borax or boric acid baits should have 5% or less boric acid or borax).
9. **Ants in your pet's food?** Draw a line of white chalk or petroleum jelly around the dish.
10. **Mop the floors** with ½ - 1 cup of borax or baking soda per gallon of hot water. **Keep crawling children off the borax cleaned floor!**
11. **Flood or drench all outside nests** with 3 gallons of warm water and 4 oz. of Safe Solutions, Inc. Enzyme Cleaner with Peppermint or carbon dioxide or carbon monoxide or diluted orange juice or steam. Be sure landscape mulch is 2" or less. Remove all debris.
12. **Ants in voids or hollow trees -** Dust with talcum powder or food-grade DE and then fill the cavity with aerosol foam insulation. Put bands of Tanglefoot ® or STP® oil treatment or petroleum jelly around the perimeter of infested trees. **Eliminate all moisture problems.**
13. **Flood or drench all outside ant nests, e.g., fire ants**, with
    a. 1 gallon of orange juice plus 2 gallons of water plus 2 tablespoons of dish soap.
    b. Several 2-liter bottles of Coca-Cola.
    c. 3 gallons of warm water and 1 - 2 oz. of Safe Solutions, Inc. Enzyme Cleaner with Peppermint.
14. **Alternative Sprays and/or Powders**
    a. Mix 10% salt and some white pepper or Tobasco® sauce in water and spray to repel ants.
    b. Blend one clove of garlic, one onion, one tablespoon of cayenne pepper and a quart of water. Steep mixture for one

hour, strain, add a tablespoon of liquid soap and spray it for ant control.

c. Wash kitchen surfaces with vinegar or baking soda solution. Sprinkle baking soda, calcium chloride, bone meal, chili powder, talcum powder, Tide® soap, and/or powdered charcoal in and around suspected points of entry.
d. Pour a line of any of the following where ants are entering the building: baking soda, calcium chlo- ride or Comet®, cinnamon, talcum or chili powder, bone meal, medicated body powder, food-grade DE, cream of tartar, red chili pepper, salt, Tide® soap, dried mint or sage, cucumber peelings, or simply draw a line of chalk.
e. Mix of 10½ oz. of water, 3 oz. of hot sauce, 1 oz. of Safe Solutions, Inc. Enzyme Cleaner with Peppermint. Spray where ants enter the home or building.
f. Spray them with virtually any cleaner you have. Create a barrier with petroleum jelly or STP® oil treatment.
g. Leaving a large piece of peanut brittle in the sun can trap literally thousands of small sweet-eating ants on the sticky surface per Howard Rustin.

15. **Other Alternative Baits**
    a. Combine: 1 part active yeast, 2 parts molasses and 1 part sugar. Mix the ingredients well. Drop a teaspoonful on several small squares of white paper. Place the paper squares along ant trails where they will not be disturbed. How does it work? The ants are attracted to the sugary feast and con-sume it readily. The action of the yeast, however, produces gas in their bellies and they can not rid themselves of it. They essentially pop. The best part of this method of alternative pest control is that it utilizes no volatile poisons which could harm you or your family or your pets.
    b. Mix ½ cup molasses and ½ cup peanut butter and 1 packet of active dry yeast.

If you are still seeing ants, 📖read <u>The Best Control</u>© or <u>The Best Control II</u>© on CD-ROM - there are many other controls available.

Good Hunting!

INTELLIGENT CONTROLS FOR BATS

Volatile, synthetic pesticide poisons are unnecessary for bat control. The best way of getting rid of bats roosting in a building is through "bat-proofing", repelling them, or exclusion by netting! They may be legally protected in your area, so you should check state and local laws before beginning any control activities.

Bat-proofing. Making a building "bat-proof" means sealing or screening all of the openings used by the bats to enter a building. It can be a difficult job because, in many cases, all upper openings 3/8 inch and larger must be sealed, but this is the only permanent method of ridding a building of bats. Use sheet metal, aluminum flashing or 1/4" hardware cloth to close entrances permanently.

Be sure there are no bats left inside before the building is sealed. Bats trapped inside may create even more of a problem than before. Pay particular attention to chimneys, cornices. louvers, shingle/shake siding, vents, warped siding and locations where the roof joins the sides and around the eaves.

June and July are peak months for bat complaints in much of the country. Unfortunately, this is the worst time of year for control. At this time, bats are rearing young in their colony. The young can not fly and stay in the roost. Bat-proofing during this period traps the young bats. They will die and rot and smell. They may also crawl and flutter into living areas.

The best time of year to bat-proof a building is either in late fall after bats have left for hibernation or in late winter and early spring before the bats arrive. If bat-proofing must be done in summer, it should be done after mid-August.

- Seal all but one or two principal openings.
- Wait 3 - 4 days for the bats to adjust to using the remaining openings.
- Then seal those openings some evening just after the bats have left for their nightly feeding.
- "Bat valves" or screens can also be used. These are placed over the remaining openings and allow the bats to leave but not to return.
- Netting (lightweight bird netting) can be used - bats will crawl out but, can not reenter.

Standard bat-proofing materials include ¼" hardware cloth, screening, sheet metal, caulking, quick setting hard putty, expanding polyurethane foam, steel wool, duct tape -the same things used for rodent proofing. Copper or large stainless steel scouring pads can be used to temporarily plug openings in tile roofs, then sealed with cement or mortar later. When old, deteriorated buildings have more openings than can be sealed economically, large sections of plastic bird netting can be draped over the roof areas of these buildings to keep out bats at a reasonable cost and thus solving most bat problems immediately.

Bat repellents. If bat-proofing is not possible, or bats need to be forced out of a building before it is bat-proofed, the bats can sometimes be repelled from their roost. At this time, only one pesticide is registered as a bat repellent. But we believe it is dangerous and should not be used. Naphthalene crystals or flakes can be spread on attic floors or placed in voids. The crystals are most effective in confined air spaces. Three to five pounds will treat an average attic, **but we do not recommend their use.**

While naphthalene may repel the bats, it vaporizes and disappears in a few weeks, and I believe is dangerous to people and pets. The bats often return. Many humans dislike the smell of naphthalene as much as bats and some people are very sensitive and should avoid all contact. Blasts of air have been used effectively to drive bats out. Lights left on will drive them away. Turn lights on and leave the lights on when they are hibernating, and they will die. Loud noise can also be used to repel bats.

Bright lights have had some success in repelling bats.

- On commercial buildings, flood lights can be pointed at the bats' entry points to keep them from entering. (Of course, the bright lights may attract insects too, which is the bats' food.)
- Attics can be illuminated with four or more bulbs or flood lights; ensure that all corners of the attic are illuminated.
- Drafts of cool air from fans and air conditioners have, on occasion, kept bats from roosting in a poorly sealed attic.
- Ultrasonic devices do not repel bats for long, so why use them? Try loud, heavy metal music.

Cleaning - Be careful to wear all of the proper clothing and protective devices and then clean up all bat droppings and then thoroughly power wash with Safe Solutions, Inc. Enzyme Cleaner with Peppermint to help remove odors, ectoparasites and the like.

Glue Boards - Denny Young has found that if you must remove a bat or colony because you suspect disease and/or other control methods have failed, you can do so quickly and safely with glue boards. Staple a glue - board directly under the entrance hole; replace every morning as needed; when you no longer have bats, seal the entrance hole.

Remember, bats are beneficial and may be legally protected in your area.

A single bat. When a single bat finds its way into a home, office, or store, it will usually find its way out again. When it cannot, capture the bat with an insect net, a coffee can, or even (as a last resort) with a gloved hand. The bat can be released and/or destroyed. Never release a sick bat or one that is not acting normally! **Never touch any wild animal or bird!**

Did you know? If you move about you scare bats and they can panic and bump into things. Bats rest from midnight to about 3 a.m., so most "invasions'" occur about 3 a.m. or just after dusk.

If you still are having bat problems, 🕮read <u>The Best Control</u>© or <u>The Best Control II</u>© on CD-ROM

INTELLIGENT CONTROLS FOR BED BUGS

INTELLIGENT PEST MANAGEMENT® CONTROL - Bed bugs are very sensitive to heat in all stages of their development. The thermal death point for the common bedbug is only 111° F. to 113° F.; even lower temperatures of 97° F. to 99° F. will kill large numbers of these bugs. Raising the temperature for an hour or so should eliminate most infestations. Use a steam cleaner to steam the cracks and crevices and mattress weekly using only tap water.

Bed bugs are also killed by prolonged exposure to low temperatures (32° F. to 48° F.) Even the eggs die at these temperatures within 30 to 50 days, although adults and nymphs die within hours. So by simply closing off an infested bedroom and leaving it unheated in cold weather can help eradicate any bed bug infestations, as will carbon dioxide fumigation of the mattress and area. Place mattress, springs, bedding, slats and frames directly in the sun or in a plastic "bag" made of heavy visquine and duct taped together with 1# - 3# of dry ice on a paper bag on top of the mattress to "fumigate the critters".

Thorough cleaning or vacuuming will help but will not completely eliminate the pests. Use a red light at night to determine where they are hiding. Caulk, foam, seal and paint all hiding areas. As a last resort, dust talcum powder, medicated body powder, food-grade diatomaceous earth or Comet® into cracks and crevices of floors and baseboards and then seal completely. Clean thoroughly using diluted Safe Solutions, Inc. Enzyme Cleaner with Peppermint and/or borax as needed.

Steam clean with the Vapor Dragon® or with Safe Solutions, Inc. Enzyme Cleaner with Peppermint and/or borax or throw out mattresses, furnishings, debris and other objects that serve as nesting sites. Routinely vacuum lint, dust and other debris from mattresses, covers and box springs. Caulk all cracks, holes, gaps and openings in walls and moldings. Re-glue all loose wallpaper. Launder and dry all linens, bedding and pads in a clothes dryer or in direct sunlight. If determined necessary later, treat bed frames, springs and mattresses with only small spot applications of talcum powder, or better yet, medicated body powder or Comet®; then as a last resort, insecticidal soap or food-grade diatomaceous earth. **Wash or spray any mattresses and/or bedding with diluted Safe Solutions, Inc. Enzyme Cleaner with Peppermint (1 oz. per quart of water) and/or 2 oz. of borax per quart of water.**

You can spot treat mattresses that must be saved at seams, folds, buttons or tears with diluted borax (½ cup per gallon of water) or better yet, with a steamer, e.g., the Vapor Dragon®, weekly. After treatment the mattress should be air dried in the sun, and then covered with plastic before use. If all else fails, carefully and lightly apply talcum powder, medicated body powder, Comet®, boric acid, food-grade diatomaceous earth dusts in any/all inaccessible areas; then caulk and/or seal and/or completely cover. Remember that thoroughness is the key to permanent bed bug control. All holes, cracks, crevices or other hiding places must be carefully sealed/caulked. Routinely wash everything with Safe Solutions, Inc. Enzyme Cleaner with Peppermint, and/or borax. Freshwater (food-grade) diatomaceous earth will control most ectoparasites of this type, but you should avoid breathing the dust. Try lightly dusting with baby powder containing talc first, but you still should avoid breathing the dust. Call 1-888-443-8738 for a Vapor Dragon®, food-grade DE or enzyme cleaners.

Duct Tape - Place duct tape, sticky-side up, around all walls and bed legs and wherever you suspect bed bug activity. You can hold the duct tape in place with masking tape on the edges.

CAUTION - Never apply volatile, residual synthetic pesticide poison sprays or dusts to an infant's, pregnant woman's, elderly person's or an invalid's mattress or anywhere people have breathing problems or are chemically sensitive. Use several applications spread (over a period of two to six weeks intervals) of diluted enzyme cleaners and/or borax, or as a last resort, some food-grade DE, but only when the label permits such usage, and only if you cannot simply throw away the infested mattress and everything else has failed to gain control.

In concluding any bed bug eradication, thoroughly inspect all attics and other possible harborage points for bats, rodents and birds. If found, clean up all guano and residue with enzymes, remove nests, spray or mist with Safe Solutions, Inc. Enzyme Cleaner with Peppermint (1 - 2 oz. per gallon of water and/or borax, ½ cup per gallon of water). If determined absolutely necessary, spot treat the area with a least-toxic food-grade DE. Caution: Wear hard hats, safety glasses, masks, gloves and wash all protective clothing and yourself thoroughly after entering any infested attics, especially any with any visible feces or guano. Clean thoroughly with Safe Solutions, Inc. Enzyme Cleaner with Peppermint and/or borax. **If you still are having bed bug problems, 🕮read The Best Control© or The Best Control II© on CD-ROM.**

INTELLIGENT CONTROLS FOR BIRDS

Birds are protected by many laws and regulations. Although pigeons, starlings, and house sparrows are not directly protected by federal law, their control is often strictly regulated by state and local governments. Public opinion is often strongly against any control measure that kills birds, even pest birds. Non-lethal bird control methods include habitat modification limiting food, water, and shelter), exclusion (with netting, porcupine wire, sticky repellents, etc.), and trapping.

Intelligent Pest Management® Bird Control Summary - (Only if you eliminate the nesting and roosting on a building, tree, statue or whatever, will you eliminate bird problems.) **Holes -** The simple closing of holes in buildings can solve many bird problems. **Nest cleanup** - Birds can nest deep in dryer vent airflow lines or other openings up to a depth of 15 feet. A simple technique to clean out the nests is to use an industrial vacuum and a flexible copper pipe to slowly pull out the nesting material; then clean the vent with diluted Safe Solutions, Inc. Enzyme Cleaner with Peppermint and close off any openings with ½" hardware cloth or place flashing around any other openings, i.e., damaged dock doors that are not in use. Once holes are blocked or netted, the birds will no longer come into the building. **Install plastic curtains or nets** on any doors that are open all day. The secret to finding the problem may be the top of the dock doors. Wherever there is a 1" or greater gap, birds are able to enter the building. Plastic netting can be used to prevent birds from constantly flying into a warehouse, landfill, court yard, etc. InterNet (1-800-328-8456) has a product line which features a selection of netting from heavy-duty grids to smaller mesh sizes to meet a variety of needs. Bird netting can be ordered in custom sizes or rolls and easily fabricated to fit most building installations and to seal off areas that attract birds. Helpful installation hints are also included in a descriptive application brochure available from InterNet. Hot Foot Mist Nets, 8' x 40', are very fine nets constructed of strong fibers that birds cannot see. The nets have a unique "pouch" construction, when the birds fly into the net, their feathers become entangled, thereby safely immobilizing them for removal. Different mesh sizes are available for birds of different sizes and the nets can be joined together to cover a greater area. If you have any questions call Hot Foot @ 1-800-533-8421. **Roosting on ledges** can be discouraged by changing the ledge angle to 45o or more. Sheet metal, Styrofoam blocks, wood, stone, etc. can be formed and fastened to ledges to achieve the desired angle.

- Building ventilators should be completely netted over using plastic netting to prevent birds from crowding their nests into ventilator slits.
- Commercial signs should all be repaired and/or screened to prevent any bird roosting space.
- All broken windows should be repaired, sealed off or screened.
- Warehouse doorways that must be left open and/or used frequently during the work day should be screened or blocked to birds by hanging clear plastic strips to the ground in front of the opening. These strips will not impede the warehouse workers' activities, but will present an impassable barrier to the eyes of any bird.
- All places or openings between window air conditioners and the building should be blocked off or screened.
- In locations where birds are utilizing palm trees for nesting sites, the frequent removal of the dead fronds from the trees will aid in eliminating bird roosting sites (as well as roof rat harborage).
- Likewise, if birds are using building vines, the vines can be removed from building sides or covered with inconspicuous plastic nets (in most cases, black is the most inconspicuous color choice).

There are four different types of bird repellents: (1) tactile (touch), (2) sound, (3) odor and (4) visual. For most urban and industrial bird problems, the tactile repellents are the most practical and effective. There are two types: (1) mechanical and (2) chemical. Porcupine wires (Nixalite™ and Cat Claw™ permanent types of mechanical repellents. They are composed of myriad spring-tempered nickel stainless steel prongs with sharp points extending outward at all angles. The prongs are fastened to a solid base which can be installed on window sills, ledges, eaves, roof peaks, ornamental architectural features or wherever birds are prone to roost. The sharp pointed wires inflict temporary discomfort, so birds avoid landing on these surfaces. All ledges and other niches must be completely covered in order for these devices to be completely effective. Wide surfaces may require two or more parallel rows of wires or strings.

Cleaning - Be careful to wear all of the proper clothing and protective devices and then clean up all bird droppings and nesting materials. Then thoroughly power wash with Safe Solutions, Inc. Enzyme Cleaner with Peppermint (1 - 2 oz. per gallon of water) to remove stains, odors, ectoparasites and the like.

If you are still having bird problems, 🕮read <u>The Best Control</u>© or <u>The Best Control II</u>© on CD-ROM.

INTELLIGENT CONTROLS FOR CHIGGERS

1. Spray the yard with diluted dish soap and vegetable oil (4 tablespoons of dish soap and 4 teaspoons of vegetable oil per gallon of water) or diluted Safe Solutions, Inc. Enzyme Cleaner with Peppermint (1 -2 oz. per gallon of water).

To treat the pain of chigger bites: rub bite with a moist aspirin tablet or put on a dab of nail polish (if you are not allergic to these).

If you still have chigger problems, 🕮read <u>The Best Control</u>© or <u>The Best Control II</u>© on CD-ROM.

INTELLIGENT CONTROLS FOR CLOTHES MOTHS AND OTHER FABRIC PESTS

These pests normally will not attack clean clothes or fabric.

1. Be sure to dry clean or wash your clothes before putting them away and they will be pest free. Thor- oughly air out dry cleaned clothing before storing in bedroom closet. The chemical odor can cause severe symptoms in some chemically sensitive individuals.**
2. Routinely clean the entire area with (1 oz. per gallon) Safe Solutions, Inc. Enzyme Cleaner with Pepper- mint or natural soaps or steam clean.

3. Mix ½ pound dried rosemary, ½ pound dried mint, ¼ pound dried ginseng and 2 tablespoons cloves and put in cheese cloth bags to be used as sachets. (You should be able to purchase these items at bulk cooking/baking supply stores or health food stores, or find someone who has an herb garden.)
4. Try sachets of any of the following: dried lemon peels, dried lavender, bay leaves, whole cloves, cedar chips, dried rosemary and mint or whole peppercorns. (Find someone who has a garden to provide the scented herbs or plant them for your own use.)
5. Lightly dust cracks and crevices lightly with food-grade DE or baking soda or talcum powder or Comet®.
6. Do not use mothballs in any closet! The Author believes mothballs contain a terribly dangerous and volatile, registered pesticide called paradichlorobenzene that does not control moths, but can harm you.

Dry cleaning fluid contains perchlorethylene, tetra or trichlorethylene which can cause serious medical symptoms in many chemically sensitive individuals. Always try to air out dry cleaned clothing, very thoroughly, prior to bringing it into your home, placing in a closet; always try to avoid putting such clothes in the bedroom. Try to find a cleaners that does not use the toxic chemicals.

If you still have problems, 🕮read <u>The Best Control</u>© or <u>The Best Control II</u>© on CD-ROM.

INTELLIGENT CONTROLS FOR COCKROACHES

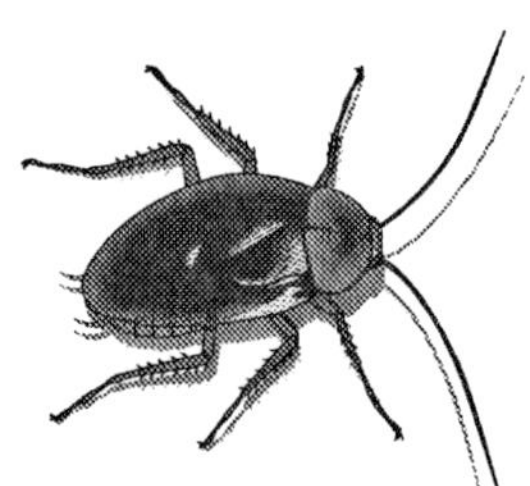

There are at least 4,000 species of cockroaches in the world and there are at least 70 described species in the U. S. with at least 41 described species in Florida, but less than 1% of the known cockroaches invade and inhabit our buildings and may become persistent, unsightly and troublesome pests. Household cockroaches are known carriers of fungi, viruses, protozoa, about 40 species of bacteria pathogenic to vertebrates and intermediate hosts for several species of helminth (flatworms). Cockroaches are considered one of the most adaptable and successful insect groups. In fact, evidence of the continual coexistence with people throughout history is testimony to how adaptable some cockroaches are to the habits of people. Cockroaches are born inebriates and omnivorous scavengers. Our buildings protect cockroaches from the weather and their natural enemies and provide them with ample sources of food and water as well as convenient places for them to hide.

Note: One pair of cockroaches can theoretically produce enough offspring in one year to carpet the floors of the average home to a depth of 1 meter per year! In August, 1997, the Journal of Economic Entomology noted: "Even with the promotion of integrated pest management programs for the German cockroach, *Blattela germanica* (L.) The pest control industry has generally relied on the use of chemically-based synthetic insecticides as the key, direct control technique in these integrated pest management (IPM) programs (Gold 1995). The financial backbone of the pest control industry for years has been the "need" for continual chemical cockroach "control."

Cockroaches have survived for more than 350 million years. Ancient fossils had the same appearance as today's cockroaches: oval and flat with long legs and antennae. The modern cockroach also has the same need for a warm, moist climate. Cockroaches are behaviorally, physiologically and genetically adaptable. While most cockroaches live wild in the tropics and sub-tropics, a few, called urban cockroaches, choose to enjoy the moist, even temperature we maintain in our homes, schools and workplaces. Cockroaches are offensive pests visually and they expel unpleasant smelling secretions that spoil the flavor of food and contaminate the air and are suspected of transporting various disease organisms in much the same way as flies. Their presence increases asthma problems. **They feed normally in packs, or aggregations.**

Note: There is a difference of opinion on the classification of cockroaches. According to many experts, cockroaches belong to the insect order Orthoptera, yet other experts consider cockroaches and praying mantids to belong to a separate order, the Dictyoptera, still others say Blattodea is the correct order but, however you classify them scientifically, everyone seems to agree they are considered to be one of our main insect pests, and a continual source of concern and embarrassment for many people!

Most cockroaches are fond of flour, German roaches prefer brown sugar or light Karo Syrup to pure sucrose and carbohydrates to proteins. They also love bread, stale beer, wine, fatty acids, alcohols, peanut butter and are attracted to ground up roaches and their own excrement. Remember this when you mix up your 5% food-grade DE/borax/boric acid/sodium borate baits - **be careful to put them out of the reach of pets, children and wildlife.**

1. Be sure all visible cracks and crevices are caulked an strong fans are left on 24 hours a day in all active areas. Remove all paper bags, cardboard and infested fiberglass insulation. Install and properly maintain fans or air conditioners and/or dehumidifier(s). **Repair or remove all moisture sources.**
2. Routinely clean or spray or mist or power wash with Safe Solutions, Inc. Enzyme Cleaner with Peppermint (1 oz. per gallon), all garbage cans and flood all garbage disposals, grease pits and all drains with the enzyme cleaner (1 oz. per

quart) as needed. Maintain routine and thorough sanitation and proper food and garbage storage. Spray, clean and completely drain all steamers or steam tables. Do not leave garbage or any food out at night! You can also rinse-and-vac and/or power wash all surfaces and cracks with Safe Solutions, Inc. Enzyme Cleaner with Peppermint (2 oz. per gallon). This will not only control the roaches, but it will also remove the roach allergens and roach smell. Caulk/seal every opening, crack or crevice you see cockroaches come out of.

3. Lightly dust with baking powder or talcum powder or medicated powder or food-grade DE or Comet® along the edges of the room and in any remaining cracks and crevices - or spray them with diluted Safe Solutions, Inc. Enzyme Cleaner with Peppermint (1 oz. per quart) or blow hot air from a hair dryer or heat gun into the cracks where you see cockroaches. **Then caulk.**
4. Mix 45% baking soda and 45% powdered sugar and 10% powdered yeast (or powdered vitamin C) and place as a bait mix. Make some 10% sucrose and 4% food-grade DE liquid baits and place them out of reach of children and pets. Place pheromone traps or duct tape (sticky-side up) wherever you see roaches. Remove all paper bags, cardboard and fiberglass insulation!
5. Spray or mist roaches with diluted Safe Solutions, Inc. Enzyme Cleaner with Peppermint (1 oz. per quart). Try spraying diluted Safe Solutions, Inc. Enzyme Cleaner with Peppermint in a power washer or steam clean. **If you control the harborage, you will control the roaches, so caulk and seal!**
6. Mop the floors with ½ cup borax per gallon of hot water. **Keep crawling children off the floor!**
7. One hour after dark, enter the room/home/building with a red/yellow light and a vacuum. Vacuum up all visible roaches before turning on the regular lights. If you are using a dry vac, add 1 teaspoon of cornstarch or talcum powder to the bag to kill the roaches. If you are using a rinse-and-vac, have some soapy or enzyme water in the container to kill the roaches. (You will take about 90% of your roach pests the first night.) Repeat once a week for several weeks or until all activity ceases. Flush or remove (or seal in plastic) all recycling materials daily.
8. Make some roach (wasp) traps by cutting the top off of a 2-liter soda pop bottle, cut in a straight line here the bottle begins to curve, put a little Vaseline around the **inside** edge (Be careful not to get any on the outside.) of the bottle and invert the top and put it back inside the bottle (like a funnel), then duct tape the edges to keep the top from falling inside and the roaches from escaping. Put some masking tape on the outside from the

bottom to the top, so the roaches can climb up and into your trap. Put some dry dog kibble or 2" - 3" of beer or wine or a piece of bread soaked in beer or a pheromone attractant (or some roach droppings) in the bottom and place under sinks, in corners, and wherever you see roaches. some roach droppings) in the bottom and place under sinks, in corners, and wherever you see roaches. You can use this trap to monitor or control. If you leave a small strip or one side open, you can visually inspect your roach trap. You can either freeze the contents or pour in diluted Safe Solutions, Inc. Enzyme Cleaner with Peppermint (1 oz. per quart of water) or hot soapy water. Empty out and reset, or throw away and make some more.

9. Create escape-proof barriers with double-sided (Mr. Sticky®) sticky tape or Vaseline® petroleum jelly or duct tape (sticky side up). You can literally trap and remove all roach problems with enough duct tape.
10. For roaches in appliances, seal the entire appliance in a plastic bag for 2 weeks; the roaches will die from dehydration, or speed up the process by filling the bag with carbon dioxide.
11. Note: Quite often a health inspector will assume you have a serious roach infestation if they see one dead cockroach in a trap, so replace traps as needed with (empty) pheromone traps.

Alternative Controls

1. Make a roach dough by combining ½ cup powdered sugar and ¼ cup shortening or bacon drippings. Add ½ cup onions, ½ cup flour and 8 oz. baking soda. (Don't forget to add some roach droppings.) Add enough water to make a dough-like consistency. Make balls of bait and put them wherever you see roaches.
2. Mix one clove garlic, one onion, one tablespoon of cayenne pepper and a quart of water. Steep for one hour, strain, add a tablespoon of liquid soap and spray it around the house for roach control.
3. Place bay leaves or talcum powder or baking soda around cracks in rooms or spray with diluted Safe Solutions, Inc. Enzyme Cleaner with Peppermint (1 oz. per quart of water).
4. If you find a roach infestation in a computer, radio, t.v., etc., simply place the entire item/appliance in a sealed plastic bag for 2 weeks. The roaches will die from dehydration.

Doug Tobias has found a new cockroach trap: Take an empty foil potato chip bag; tape it against the wall. The odor will attract roaches so they will enter the bag but the oil residue on the foil will prevent their escape.

If you are still seeing roaches, 🕮read The Best Control© or The Best Control II© on CD-ROM - there are many other controls available.

- ☎ **Contact Get Set, Inc., @ 1-616-677-1261 for The Best Control© or The Best Control II©,**
  🖳 **web site: www.getipm.com or**
- ☎ **Safe Solutions, Inc. @ 1-888-443-8738 for Safe Solutions, Inc. Enzyme Cleaner with Peppermint and food-grade DE, 🖳 web site: www.safesolutionsinc.com**

INTELLIGENT CONTROLS FOR CRICKETS - THE NOISY COCKROACH

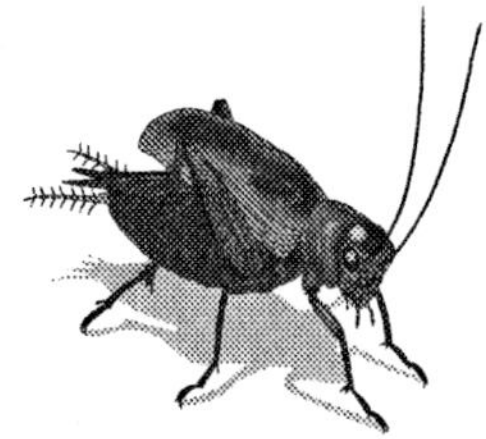

Be sure all doors, windows and screens fit tightly. Cracks and other openings from the outside (especially near ground level) that provide access into the building should be sealed. Also, caulk or otherwise seal cracks and crevices inside the building that provide hiding places. Use a strong vacuum or roach sticky traps or boric acid baits to control areas, e.g., behind or under heavy furniture and appliances or in other inaccessible areas. Weeds and debris around the outside of the building should be closely mowed and/or removed to eliminate their normal habitats. Change outside lighting to sodium vapor lights or yellow incandescent lights that are less attractive to crickets (and other insects). Remove feeding and breeding sites outside. Garbage and other refuse that serves as food should be stored in containers with tight lids and elevated off the ground on platforms or bricks.

Cricket infestations are usually seasonal. Most often problems occur during the fall as evenings become cooler and the insects seek to enter your building for warmth and shelter. Because of this, occasional vacuuming or applications of diluted Safe Solutions, Inc. Enzyme Cleaner with Peppermint or baits containing 3% - 5% borax, food-grade DE or duct tape (placed sticky-side up) are all that is usually all that is needed indoors for adequate cricket control. Crickets require a steady supply of fresh water and will drown easily in a shallow dish with a few pieces of dry dog food put in a shot glass in the middle of the saucer. Grasshoppers can be controlled outside with semaspore baits which spread an infection from which they cannot recover.

You can make your own bait with corn meal and (1% - 5%) sodium borate or borax or food-grade DE. Try spraying diluted borax or food-grade DE directly on the problem area/bait/pest.

Be careful not to contaminate anything (especially plants) with borax. Remember that we have quickly and safely controlled crickets in the lab and field simply with 1 oz. per quart of water Safe Solutions, Inc. Enzyme Cleaner with Peppermint. You can also steam clean/kill them. **Routinely mow your yard.**

A thorough inspection should be made and properly recorded first. Correctly identify the species. Note all in infestations and conditions and conditions conducive. Vacuum up any invaders inside or outside. Cricket control begins outdoors with the reduction or elimination of moist harborage near the structure, such as removal of bricks, firewood, stone, lumber, wood piles and other debris. Routinely mow your yard and keep all of your shrubs and gardens free of weeds and organic debris. Tightly seal and routinely clean garbage cans with Safe Solutions, Inc. Enzyme Cleaner with Peppermint and borax; stand them on bricks or blocks (off the ground). Repair all leaking plumbing and moisture problems inside and outside your building.

Crawl spaces should be well ventilated and dry; the installation of a dehumidifier and/or a poly/vapor barrier and vents will help. Seal all entry points such as door thresholds by installing doorsweeps; caulk or seal or screen holes in masonry, around pipes, wires, facia, soffits, vents, trims, windows and doors and all visible cracks and crevices outside and inside. Eliminate all leaking plumbing, route downspouts away from the foundation. Lightly dust with talcum or medicated body powder or finely ground calcium chloride. Maintain proper grade drainage, install vapor barriers in crawls and install air conditioning dehumidifiers and/or fans.

Some crickets, e.g., field and house and sometimes ground crickets, are attracted to lights...so shut them off or change outdoor lighting to less attractive sodium vapor lamps or yellow bulbs. Place glue boards in and around entrances. Use 5% food-grade DE or borax and molasses baits, but try baking soda, Comet®, talcum powder or medicated body powder first. Remember, crickets can be found anywhere, especially where food, clothes, linens and books are stored and it is especially vital not to contaminate these items with any toxic poisons. It is far better to take the time to use silicone caulk, patching plaster, mortar, cement, foam insulation, etc. to permanently seal all cracks, crevices and other openings; to use a hammer and nails or screw driver and screws to permanently tighten all siding, trim, molding, framing, etc.; plumbing tools to correct all leaks and to clean up and permanently remove all cricket populations, harborages, food and moisture sources than to poison even one person...besides, you have to do this maintenance eventually anyway! Clean or simply spray infested areas with Safe Solutions, Inc. Enzyme Cleaner with Peppermint (1 oz. per quart of water), or a steam cleaner and/or borax (½ cup per gallon of water).

Spray crickets with Safe Solutions, Inc. Enzyme Cleaner with Peppermint (1 oz. per quart of water) and they will die quickly. You can make your own baits using any food source the crickets seem to prefer, but these baits must be placed only where people, pets and/or wildlife can not reach them. Try corn meal sprayed or mixed with a water solution containing 1% - 5% borax or lightly dusted with food-grade DE and place in out of the way areas - away from people, pets and wildlife. Sprinkle baking soda, Comet®, talcum or medicated body powder in infested areas- vacuum everything up when control is accomplished.

Diluted Safe Solutions, Inc. Enzyme Cleaner with Peppermint enzymes at a rate of 1 oz. per quart of water kills 100% of the crickets in about 10 seconds. Dish soap at 1 oz. per quart of water kills them all in 35 seconds. Vinegar in water (at 4 oz. per quart) kills crickets in about a minute. Salt water will kill about 50% in about a minute. Lemon juice in water (4 oz. per quart) will kill about 80% in about a minute.

Good luck with the noisy cockroach! If you are still having problems with crickets, 🕮read The Best Control© or The Best Control II© on CD-ROM.

INTELLIGENT CONTROLS FOR DUST MITES

The term "house dust mites" has been applied to a large number of sightless, eight-legged, microscopic arachnids called mites (smaller than a speck of salt) found in dwellings associated with dust. About 80% of dust in a building is us; each one of us sheds several million cells daily or about the weight of a paper clip. A family of four could fill a quart container in a month! Dust mites breathe through their skin and have a hypopial stage that makes them virtually immune to synthetic insecticide poisons and fumigants during this deep dormancy stage of life. They love warm, humid settings and feed on skin scales and dander shed by humans and animals.

Hundreds can be found in one pinch of dust. Household dust is a microscopic blend of sloughed skin cells, sneezed viruses, soil, furniture and clothing fibers, pet dander, carpeting pieces, soil, mold, bacteria, insect fragments, etc. The average U. S. home collects 40 pounds of dust per year, which is home to at least 15 species of mites that live about 45 days and one ounce can contain over 42,000 individuals.

ECONOMIC IMPORTANCE: 35 million people in the U. S. suffer from dust mite allergy symptoms. In England, 1/3 of all cereal foods inspected had dust mite contaminations. Because of the medical implications, house dust and the fauna of mites associated with house dust have been tested for the source of the house dust allergen. The highest house dust allergen activity was found in dust samples stored at 85% RH. Mite allergens are mainly present in feces of house dust mites and may become airborne and inhaled by patients giving rise to asthma, rhinitis, or atopic dermatitis. Mite cultures contain so much allergen that a millionth of one per cent is still reactive to allergic people per Judith A. Mollet of Virginia Tech. This is suburbia's most common allergen. The second most common allergen is the pet cat whose dander, hair and saliva are all allergens. In the Northeast the cockroach is the most important allergen. Even the most spotless buildings house millions of dust mites. It is estimated that humans shed about 400,000 particles of skin a minute!

DISTRIBUTION: Nearly cosmopolitan, associated with house dust, bedding, carpets, furniture and bird nests.

HOSTS: Mammals, particularly man, and in bird nests and occasionally in bee hives.

DESCRIPTION: A sightless, microscopic (1/100 of an inch long) creature that lives in carpeting, drapes, bedding, upholstered furniture and stuffed toys. They prefer temperatures in the 68° - 84° F. range. Both male and female adult house dust mites are globular in shape, creamy white and have a striated cuticle. The female measures approximately 420 microns in length and 320 microns in width. The male is approximately 420 microns long and 245 microns wide. (About the size of a sharp pencil dot. They look like miniature hairy dinosaurs, complete with armor plates and pincers.)

Adults are about 1/100" to 1/64" long with soft, oval, somewhat flattened bodies. They are very dependent on temperature, moisture and an adequate food supply. While these microscopic mites, which are relatives of spiders that feed on our dead (moldy) skin, are found in the United States, they are much more prevalent in England where humidity is very high (over 50%), so use a dehumidifier and a fan with an activated charcoal filter. You provide their food in the form of dead skin cells that fall off your body each day. As Heywood Banks, the singing comedian, has written in a song, "Those dust mites smack their bony lips and eat that skin like taco chips. It's a rain of manna from the sky." **Dust mites are easily controlled when they are exposed to direct sunlight so hang your wash out on a clothesline or steam clean all items.**

House dust mites often cause allergic reactions. Dust mite feces contain at least 15 proteins that act as allergens. These mites and/or their droppings may cause allergic reactions to 500 million people worldwide and be responsible for triggering reactions in 50% to 80% of asthmatics! The University of Virginia estimates hospital emergency rooms see over 200,000 asthmatics a year with allergic reactions to dust mites. Female house dust mites can deposit 50 eggs in her 36 day (average) life span. Each mite can deposit 20 fecal pellets a day. So you can see how they can totally overwhelm your area very quickly with allergens that are normally "recycled" every time you vacuum or dust. For more information call 1-800-7-ASTHMA and 1-800-422-DUST.

DUST MITE SPECIES: There are several species worldwide including the House Dust Mite, Euroglyphus maynei, the American House Dust Mite, *Dermatophagoides farinae* (Hughes) and the European House Dust Mite *Dermatophagoides pteronyssinus* (Trouessart). Cast skins, fluids, feces and body parts of house dust mites accumulate with other dust and small household allergenic disintegrated matter. Vacuum with a Hepa filter intensely. A new and effective control method is to spray carpet with tannic acid solutions obtained from carpet cleaning suppliers. We prefer that you mop and routinely clean/dust and/or use a rinse-and-vac with diluted Safe Solutions, Inc. Enzyme Cleaner with Peppermint.

LIFE STAGES AND BIOLOGY: The life cycle of 2 mite species *D. farinae* (Hughes) and *D. pteronyssinus* (Trouessart) include egg, active larvae, resting larva (pharate tritonymph), active tritonymph, resting tritonymph (pharate adult), and active adult. Between 19-30 days are needed to complete a life cycle depending upon the temperature and humidity (Furumizo, 1973). Mated females live about 2 months. A male may attach itself to a tritonymph female and mate when she reaches the adult stage. *D. farinae* lays eggs over a 30-day period, producing about an egg a day, while *D. pteronyssinus* lays about 80 eggs over a 45 day period. There is a general agreement that house mites in the home feed on shed skin of man. The average individual sheds 0.5 to 1.0 gram of skin daily. Each dust mite can excrete 20 fecal pellets in a day, or an amount of excrement equal to 200 times its own weight in a lifetime. Spieksma et al. (1971) reported that the mites were very sensitive to relative humidity and at 60% or lower the mite population stops growing and dies out, so **install a dehumidifier and fans.** Safe Solutions, Inc. Enzyme Cleaner with Peppermint will control not only the dust mites but the fungus *Aspergillus repens* which predigests human skin flakes into a form the mites can eat.

Non-Toxic Control:

1. **Reduce the relative humidity with properly installed dehumidifiers, fans and/or air conditioners.** Routinely remove (if possible) any dander, dead skin and/or dust and/or dust catching materials, e.g., books, magazines, clutter, stuffed animals, rugs, textiles, furs, feathers, woolens, drapes, carpets, etc. and/or enclose mattresses, pillows, and box springs in plastic and clean and/or wash or spray all surfaces and air filters with Safe Solutions, Inc. Enzyme Cleaner with Peppermint as needed. Install allergen trapping filters in air conditioning/heating systems. Keep all clothing in closets with the doors closed. Keep windows closed in the spring. **Clean the air with HEPA air filtration**.
2. **Avoid sleeping with or keeping pets** - especially cats and dogs or wash often with 1 - 2 oz. of Safe Solutions, Inc. Enzyme Cleaner with Peppermint. It is best to keep your pets outside; if you can not, HEPA vacuum daily and wash your hands after petting your pet. **Dander stays around long after the pet has gone**.
3. **Keep windows and doors closed and as weather-tight as much as possible** to avoid the entry of pollen and insects. Clean window coverings every two weeks or replace with shades or mini-blinds.
4. **Keep food products in glass containers and control all insect pests.**
5. **Reduce the relative humidity below 50%;** repair all plumbing/moisture problems; install a dehumidifier and/or air filtration system. Hot air vents should be covered with HEPA filters.
6. **Avoid wet mopping and dusting** unless you use diluted Safe Solutions, Inc. Enzyme Cleaner with Peppermint (1 oz. per

gallon of water). Then use Safe Solutions, Inc. Enzyme Cleaner with Peppermint in a rinse-and-vac or spray diluted Safe Solutions, Inc. Enzyme Cleaner with Peppermint, but vacuum very thoroughly with a rinse-and-vac, vacuum with a HEPA filter at least once a week - go very slowly and allow the vacuum to actually suck up all materials; dust furniture and shelves before you vacuum. Carefully and slowly vacuum beds, pillows, drapes, carpet, upholstered furniture, floors etc. Steam clean everything. Don't allow smoking in the building.

7. **Shampoo or steam clean or dry clean (off premises and air out thoroughly before returning)** or better yet, simply put in to the sun all non-washable carpets at least one a year.
8. **Weekly washing** sheets, pillows, rugs and carpets in soapy water or borax at least 122$_o$ F. for 5 - 8 minutes will kill all mites.
9. **Direct sunlight** also kills mites and bedding is the prime harborage for dust mites, with stuffed furniture a close second. So put furniture, bedding, drapes, clothing, etc. out in the sun and/or line dry your washing. Replace heavy drapes with washable shades, mini-blinds or lightweight curtains.
10. **Put plush toys in a plastic bag,** tie the bag and freeze for 24 hours. Repeat as needed, e.g.. once a week or wash them weekly. It is best to only purchase washable stuffed toys and wash them weekly with Safe Solutions, Inc. Enzyme Cleaner with Peppermint in water (100$_o$ - 120$_o$ F.).
11. **To control dust and dust mite allergens take a (square box) window fan, using duct tape attach two (charcoal) furnace filters (cut to size) to the fan grills on both the intake and exhaust sides.** Turn on the fan to filter the air. Activated charcoal will increase the filtration results and help remove odors and some toxic gases. Change filters as needed. You can also use a high-efficiency HEPA air cleaner.
12. **Over 25% of an old pillow might be dust and dust mites** - so get a new one every 6 months. Remove carpeting, rugs, stuffed animal toys and drapes if needed.

Least-toxic Control:

13. **Routinely steam clean and/or mop and clean with Safe Solutions, Inc. Enzyme Cleaner with Peppermint or alcohol.** Then, if you still have any allergic reactions, as a last resort, you may have to try to clean with borax (½ cup per gallon of hot water). Houses severely infested with dust mites might require more cleaning with Safe Solutions, Inc. Enzyme Cleaner with Peppermint and/or borax to reduce mite allergens to tolerable levels (less than two micrograms of allergen per gram of dust).

14. **Clean any mold in the basement, bathrooms, kitchen, etc. with diluted bleach or borax or, better yet, with 2 oz. of Safe Solutions, Inc. Enzyme Cleaner with Peppermint per gallon of water.**

MORE METHODS TO MANAGE DUST MITE ALLERGIES - Caution: Children's bedrooms may be hazardous to their health. Kids occupy them a third or more of each day, and while there, come in close, long-term contact with bedding, carpeting and other fibers. While these furnishings can be comforting touches, they also contain most allergy sufferers' biggest enemies: dust mites. Microscopic arachnids, these 8-legged spider-like scavengers thrive in humid and warm conditions, shedding particles that trigger symptoms even after the insects cease to exist. Remove the fuzzies - wool blankets and non-washable stuffed toys. Install medical-grade air cleaners, use dustless vacuums and obtain other less costly aids that keep allergies at bay. Humans shed about 1/5 oz. on dead skin (dander) every week. About 80% of the "dust" seen "floating" in a sunbeam is actually shed skin flakes. Dust mites can only eat dead skin flakes (both animal and human) that have fungus growing on them. Safe Solutions, Inc. Enzyme Cleaner with Peppermint (1 - 2 oz.) and/or borax (½ cup) per gallon of water kill the fungus and eliminate their food source and also kill dust mites.

The first hurdle to overcome: The bed. That's because a mattress is the resort capital of the dust mite's world. A double bed mattress can hold millions of mites; you feed them with you and your provide them with about 1 pint of moisture vapor each night through your breathing and perspiration. Pillows and blankets are popular too. Mattresses and box springs should be encased in zippered, dust-proof covers. Sleep movement (people toss and turn up to 60 times each night) kicks up allergens, which are then breathed in and/or can remain suspended in the air for up to 24 hours. Washing bed linens in hot water is crucial. Water below 120_o F. prevents accidental scalding, but it must be 130_o F. or you must use borax and/or Safe Solutions, Inc. Enzyme Cleaner with Peppermint in cooler water to kill dust mites. For hotter water without scalds, get an "instant flow" device that supplies hot water at a specific point of use, such as a washer. Because bunks, canopies and upholstered headboards attract dust, avoid them, and don't allow a bed to be placed on the floor as it fosters dampness because bedding can't breathe, and dampness means moisture - an ideal condition for mites. Try leaving an electric blanket turned on high during the day to dry the humidity and kill the dust mites in the mattress. Wash blankets in hot water and borax every two weeks. **Avoid blankets made of wool or down or routinely wash them in 2 oz. of Safe Solutions, Inc. Enzyme Cleaner with Peppermint and/or 2 oz. of borax per gallon of water.**

The next place to concentrate on is the floor. Mites claim it as private stomping grounds too. The University of Virginia maintains that carpets are likely to have 100 times more allergens than wood floors. Besides hardwood, tile and vinyl are good flooring alternatives. You will still need to remove traces of dust on them and on woodwork, however, by cleaning with water and Safe Solutions, Inc. Enzyme Cleaner with Peppermint, then wax or oil regularly. Even using a damp cloth with diluted Safe Solutions, Inc. Enzyme Cleaner with Peppermint or diluted alcohol every day helps. Small rugs and throws, if they are washable - and laundered often in borax - are all right. Low pile carpet usually is not as troublesome to an allergy sufferer as high shag. A vacuum with a high-efficiency particular air (HEPA) filter will capture particles without spewing exhaust dust, as a standard vacuum's paper filters does. A HEPA filter eliminates 99% of dust. There are chemical carpet products that reduce or destroy allergens - A moist powder is sold in all states but California. A tannic acid spray is acceptable there. A central or portable air purifier with a HEPA or electrostatic filter will remove particles and some dust mites - Keep in mind it is only effective on airborne irritants.

A refrigerated air conditioning system which, if ducts are professionally and routinely cleaned, can prevent hot and humid conditions that stimulate mite growth. Central heating ducts demand similar maintenance and synthetic filters to prevent dirt particles. Keep indoor relative humidity below 50% by using a dehumidifier, especially during humid seasons. Pets: Animal dander, saliva and other irritants, including dust that their fur collects, may cause allergic reactions, so keep them out of bedrooms or use an air filter.

Windows: Choose washable curtains or roller shades over draperies or blinds. When you clean, move all furniture to the center of the room so you can reach all of the corners and, with a damp cloth, wipe all of the moldings, light fixtures, shelves and door and window tops. Clean wood or linoleum floors daily with a specially treated dust cloth and mop cover. Don't use dusters, dust mops. bag-equipped vacuum cleaners or brooms - these utensils merely rearrange the dust or provide breeding grounds for additional dust mite/allergen growth.

Medical-grade air filters circulate and effectively clean up to 300 cu. ft. of air per minute. Inexpensive table top models generally are ineffective. 30 drops of tea tree oil in your sprayer, washing machine or rinse-and-vac will kill mold and dust mites. The distinct tea tree odor disappears when dry. Air out for 1 - 2 hours before re-entry. Repeat as needed. Metabolic gases emitted from molds and fungi growing inside buildings may be a significant source of volatile organic compounds (VOC's) that can cause indoor air quality problems known collectively as the "sick building syndrome". Spray or wash with 1 oz. Safe Solutions, Inc. Enzyme Cleaner with Peppermint per gallon of water. Tape an activated charcoal filter on both sides of a window fan - turn on and filter mites/dust from the air. Change filters as needed. Install and properly maintain dehumidifiers and/or air conditioning. Lower the relative humidity below 50% and control this pest. **Remove all dust and dead skin routinely and thoroughly.**

If you are still having problems with dust mites, 🕮read The Best Control© or The Best Control II© on CD-ROM.

INTELLIGENT CONTROLS FOR EARWIGS

Earwigs are conspicuous and easily recognized relatives of cockroaches. They are ¼ - 1" long, elongated, flattened insects with forceps or pinchers at the tail end; they may be winged or wingless. At first glance, winged earwigs appear to be wingless; in fact, their wings fold up many times under the small front wing covers; some fly to lights. Earwigs have chewing mouthparts and are opportunistic omnivores that feed on other insects and often scavenge in garbage and moist plant material. They also feed on some plant tissue, and at least one is a pest in greenhouses. They are dependent on high moisture. Earwigs are active at night; they shelter together and are quiet during the day, hiding in moist, shady locations. Tarsi are 3 segmented.

Earwig females tend their young. Like roaches, they are crack and crevice oriented. They place their eggs in moist depressions or holes, guard them, groom them until they hatch, and take care of the early stage nymphs. Earwigs grow with gradual/simple metamorphosis: older nymphs and adults harbor together - their gregarious behavior is (like the cockroach) the result of an aggregation pheromone.

Approximately 1,100 species of earwigs have been described worldwide. About 22 species occur in the U. S., but only a few are household pests. The common name of "earwig" comes from an old European superstition that these insects enter the ears of sleeping people and bore into the brain. The old Anglo-Saxon word earwicga literally means "ear-creature". This belief is basically without foundation; only occasionally one will try to hide inside a human ear. Dermaptera refers to the "skin-like" forewings present in winged species, and the term forficulina translates into "little scissors." Antennae are thread-like and about half the body length. The forceps-like abdominal cerci are apparently used as both offensive and defensive warnings or weapons, and are sometimes used to capture prey and to fold their wings after flight. As frightening as they look these pincers are not considered harmful to people. They are considered to be beneficial insects by many people because they are predators on some small insects, e.g., aphids, and they are primarily scavengers of dead animal or plant materials, although they do feed on and/or damage live plant materials. Populations generally build up around building foundations. If you must kill them simply spray the foundation with dish soap water and/or diluted Safe Solutions, Inc. Enzyme Cleaner with Peppermint (1 - 2 oz. per gallon of water). **Properly install and use a dehumidifier and/or air conditioner and/or fans.**

- Vacuum basement areas or elsewhere inside or outside to remove earwigs.

- See the "inspection" traps. Add a little honey or peanut butter (and a little earwig frass), bury or place a shallow dish, bottle, jar, or an empty tuna/sardine can in the earth - so the "hole" is now at ground level - add or leave a little fish oil in your "trap" - in the early a.m. shake the contents of each "trap" into a bucket of soapy water. You can also make shallow traps with soapy or diluted Safe Solutions, Inc. Enzyme Cleaner with Peppermint.
- Properly install a dehumidifier and fans to establish a low moisture zone around the building.
- Prepare a band of vegetation-free (and bark/mulch-free) area around the building.
- Caulk/seal all cracks and crevices in the foundation. Lightly dust with Comet® or talcum or medicated body powder or food-grade DE.
- Sprays of detergents and/or dish soaps are known to quickly kill earwigs. Use pesticidal soaps when labeled for this use, or better still spray with diluted Safe Solutions, Inc. Enzyme Cleaner with Pepper- mint (1 - 2 oz. per gallon of water).
- Bait with 5% or less boric acid or food-grade DE in corn meal lightly coated with corn oil - don't forget to add a little earwig frass. **Keep all baits out of the roach of children, pets and wildlife.**
- Earwigs will not cross a stripe of petroleum jelly or duct tape placed sticky-side up.
- A tachnid fly parasite imported from Europe will greatly reduce earwig populations. Plant dill, parsley, sweet clover, fennel, buckwheat and herbs to make these flies feel at home.
- Leave a couple of cans (half full of beer) out overnight - tomorrow they may be full of earwigs.
- Steam clean the infested area.

If you still are having earwig problems, 🕮read The Best Control© or The Best Control II© on CD-ROM.

INTELLIGENT CONTROLS FOR FLEAS

Adult fleas are truly the "vampires" of the insect world because they feed only on our blood and the blood of our pets. They are narrow, small, wingless insects, red, brown or black in color and are protected by a hard flat shell. They are hard to see and even harder to kill with volatile pesticide poisons - so why use poison? When you try to find this tiny (1/32" - 1/3") invader, remember to check your pet closely behind the ears, at the base of tail, on the stomach and between the toes. The flea has armor-like plates in layers - each with backward pointing spikes (or spines) so they can move easily and quickly through hair or feathers.

Their feet have double claws for holding on to their host and they also have a barbed "mustache" under their mouth to further anchor them to the skin as they feed with their piercing-sucking mouth parts.

Their bites cause an inflammation of the skin and can carry disease and parasites. Fleas can pull up to 400 times their own weight. Fleas literally "fly" with their hind legs; they can jump 150-200 times their body length (the equivalent of a man jumping 1,400-1,800 feet!) Behind their legs is a rubbery-muscular protein that allows them to move against gravity 135 times faster than you or me. After its lift-off, the flea cartwheels end over end, until it reaches its new host/meal. One pair of mating fleas living for nine months can theoretically produce a quarter of a million little "vampires", or up to one trillion offspring in a year! To the voracious little flea, dogs, cats, birds, humans or even elephants are simply something to eat.

Frequently launder pet bedding and rugs that pets frequent in hot, soapy water and dry in a clothes dryer or direct sunlight. Steam clean, vacuum or rinse-and-vac carpets with Safe Solutions, Inc. Enzyme Cleaner with Peppermint (1 oz. per gallon of water) and/or borax (½ cup per gallon of water) thoroughly to remove lint and dust around baseboards and cracks where flea eggs and larvae accumulate. Eliminate vegetation that will harbor native mammals and/or rodents. Prevent pets from resting under the building, and exclude wild mammals by screening attic and eaves entrances. Thoroughly clean furniture in areas that pets tend to frequent and use. Wash frequently using Safe Solutions, Inc. Enzyme Cleaner with Peppermint. Most research shows adult fleas rarely leave the host (the primary environment); the second environment is the carpet/floor or nest/burrow which contains the majority of the flea eggs, larvae and pupae. You must control both environments to control the flea infestation.

The secret to flea population management is the flea's life cycle; the adult must contribute timely nourishment for larvae under special conditions or the young will not survive. No longer a regional problem, today fleas are common in all parts of the country except very dry areas (so install a dehumidifier). The most important and common species that you must manage is the cat flea which feeds on a variety of hosts, including cats, dogs, rodents, foxes, opossums and humans. This flea prefers pets and will not affect humans unless populations are excessive or the pet is removed from its resting areas. The situation that occurs when families remove the pet, take a vacation, then return home to find ravenous fleas is not uncommon. **An outline of the sequence of events:**

- A summertime vacation assures good flea-growing conditions (temperature and humidity).
- Taking the pet with you removes the main host/food supply for your fleas.
- While the family is away, flea larvae continue to develop, feeding on dried blood; pupae complete their cycle and are ready to emerge; flea adults become ravenous.

- The family returns to the adult fleas emerged and emerging - ready to feed and accept ALL available warm-blooded hosts - (you).
- Before you go inspect inside - put your pant legs inside your socks and wrap duct tape (sticky-side out) around your lower legs.

Fleas belong to insect order Siphonaptera. They are tiny wingless insects that undergo complete metamorphosis, having egg, larval, pupal and adult stages. There are over 2,400 described flea species in the world, 95% of these are parasites of mammals; the remaining species parasitize birds. Over $6.6 billion is spent (totally) by pet owners trying and trying and trying to get rid of fleas just in the U. S.! The fight has been going on a long time - W. Colas in his book Adam in Eden: or Natures Paradise published in 1657, noted that "water in which rue *(Ruta)* has been soaked, if scattered about the house, will drive away fleas and kill them."

Doris Rapp, M.D. has noted:
Do not use typical flea or tick pesticide collars, shampoos or powders or No Pest Strips. Some of these can be associated with an increased incidence of cancer and birth defects.
If pregnant women use these, the chance of brain cancer in their children is doubled.

1. Wash pets in Not Nice to Fleas® or 1 - 2 oz. of Safe Solutions, Inc. Enzyme Cleaner with Peppermint as needed. Steam clean or vacuum thoroughly every day for two weeks and/or mop with 1 cup of borax per gallon or wash or rinse-and-vac floors or spray with diluted Safe Solutions, Inc. Enzyme Cleaner with Peppermint. Use a steam cleaner weekly to clean carpets, floors and furniture. If you spray carpet with 1 gallon of a 2% solution of borax, boric acid or sodium borate per 2,000 sq. feet - and then respray with another gallon of hot water you take the toxic material (crystals) down to the nap. Note: Borax laundry powder may stain or cause rust.) **Keep infants off borax treated floors**.
2. Mop the floors with 1 oz. per gallon or spray 1 oz. per quart Safe Solutions, Inc. Enzyme Cleaner with Peppermint and/or 1 cup borax per gallon of water. Spray yards and crawls with 1 oz. per quart Safe Solutions, Inc. Enzyme Cleaner with Peppermint or plain salt water **(borax and/or salt water will also kill plants).**
3. The oldest form of flea control was to catch the flea, place it between your thumbnail and forefinger nail and press until you heard a nice pop. As each flea female can lay one egg an hour, this may not be a very practical or "easy" job.

4. Steam clean and/or rinse-and-vac with diluted Safe Solutions, Inc. Enzyme Cleaner with Peppermint and/or borax. This will remove dried blood, carpet fibers and other debris, diluted excrement, flea larva and their silk, eggs, pupal cocoons, adults, feces and other food sources. Carpet is the perfect flea environment!
5. Spray pets with (1 oz. per quart) Safe Solutions, Inc. Enzyme Cleaner with Peppermint or bath them in Not Nice to Fleas® (is Nice to Pets) or 1 - 2 oz. of Safe Solutions, Inc. Enzyme Cleaner with Pepper- mint and wash bedding weekly in Safe Solutions, Inc. Enzyme Cleaner with Peppermint and/or borax.
6. Use a hose-end sprayer and spray the yard with nematodes or with (1 - 2 oz. per gallon) Safe Solutions, Inc. Enzyme Cleaner with Peppermint to control outside flea sources. Note: 90% of opossums in urban Midwest areas are infected with fleas. Hot summer temperatures (especially when dry) normally prevent fleas from developing. **Only shady and moist areas need to be sprayed. Spray crawl spaces with salt water - be careful not to spray nails and/or any iron surfaces or ferrous metals.**

If you are still seeing fleas, 🕮read The Best Control© or The Best Control II© on CD-ROM; there are many other alternative controls available.

INTELLIGENT CONTROLS FOR FLIES

Flies belong to the insect order Diptera and are related to mosquitoes and gnats. Of the more than 700,000 known species of insects, well over 110,000 are flies. Diptera means two ("di") wings ("ptera"), and it is on the basis of this single characteristic (one pair of wings) that all the species of flies are grouped together. As stated, Diptera literally means "two-winged" and, indeed, only the front pair of wings are functional and they are clear and membranous. The hind wings are represented by a pair of small knob-like or club-shaped organs called halteres or balancers. These small, vibrating structures aid in flying and are in place of a second pair of wings. The vibrating halteres have their own set of control muscles that are controlled by the fly's visual system. Without them flies tumble and crash; with them, they can change course without a wobble in less than 30 milliseconds - and make the fly extremely hard to swat. The adult fly does not possess mandibles, but the mouthparts are modified into a proboscis for sponging/lapping or piercing and sucking. Flies are cold-blooded insects that move about looking for external heat sources; most flies are diurnal and are attracted to certain wavelengths of light. Flies buzz around windows and can be easily vacuumed up by windows or lights. Most flies have large compound eyes and usually three simple eyes. Each of the fly's compound eyes has about 4,000 six-sided lenses - so they can detect the slightest movement. Flies taste with their feet. The larvae or maggot is legless and the head is often reduced or indistinguishable and retracted into the thoracic segments. The two-winged flies constitute a larger order of insects and well over 110,000 different species are known throughout the world. This group forms one of the most highly specialized of insect orders and many species are of the utmost significance in regard to human welfare. **If there is anything as "harmless as a fly", it is certainly not the common housefly or any of its relatives.**

Diseases, e.g., malaria, dysentery, sleeping sickness, onchocerciasis, elephantiasis and yellow fever are carried or transmitted from man to man by bloodsucking dipterous flies. Many other diseases are transmitted mechanically by flies due to the habit exhibited by many species of sucking liquid from excreta and other decaying organic matter and then settling on and vomiting on your food.

The fly was made to distribute quantities of pathogenic disease organisms. Its 6 feet are equipped with bristles and sticky pads and its proboscis is hairy. A sticky liquid comes out of the hollow hairs on their feet allowing them to walk upside down and on glass, etc. The fly's digestive tract is an incubator for germs! My mother began to teach me IPM control when I was a very young boy. She said, "Shut the door you are letting in the flies!" This is still good advice - even better is to have a second entry door as an extra barrier against fly invasion.

All flies pass through four distinct stages of their life cycle: egg, larva, pupa and adult (complete metamorphosis). The synanthropic (attracted to habitats) filth flies look for any warm, filthy, moist environment in which to lay their eggs, since their larvae feed and grow under these conditions. An adult female housefly may lay up to 2,400 eggs in her lifetime, singly or in groups. More than a thousand flies and 2,000 maggots a week can be produced in just one dirty garbage can! Fly larvae, called maggots, have a wide range of feeding habits depending on the species. Some larvae feed on plants and can be serious agricultural pests. Others feed on rotting or decaying plants or animals, or on animal excrement. Maggots of other species are internal parasites of arthropods or vertebrates. Most adult flies are winged and fly readily.

As stated previously, flies and all other dipterans only have one pair of wings, as opposed to other orders of winged insects, e.g., bees, termites, moths, etc. which have two pairs. Routinely steam clean or spray/clean/mist all infested areas with Safe Solutions, Inc. Enzyme Cleaner with Peppermint and/or borax.

Of the five most serious diseases in the world, flies, including mosquitoes, spread the organisms that are responsible for four: Malaria, sleeping sickness, Leishmaniasis and filarasis. They also are responsible for spreading yellow fever, typhoid, parathpoid, bacillary dysentery, pinworms, roundworms, whipworms, hookworms and tapeworms and various diarrheal illnesses. In the United States, the toll of the worst afflictions - heart attacks, cancer and strokes - is annually numbered in the thousands; in the tropics, the dead and disabled from fly borne diseases are counted by the millions. In the United States flies are considered more annoying than dangerous, but as recently as the turn of the 20th century, malaria and typhoid were major health problems. The activity of flies is a nuisance and the accumulation of dead adults is a respiratory hazard for many people. **A well fed fly defecates at least once every 5 minutes! So routinely clean with Safe Solutions, Inc. Enzyme Cleaner with Peppermint (1 oz. per gallon of water)!**

1. Use a fly swatter or, better yet, simply vacuum up all visible flies.
2. Routinely clean with 1 oz. of Safe Solutions, Inc. Enzyme Cleaner with Peppermint per gallon of water. Institute proper food and garbage storage.
3. Daily empty and clean all food handling equipment, dishes and garbage containers and daily remove and/or bury all droppings, fruit and organic debris inside and/or outside.
4. Add (1 oz. per quart) Safe Solutions, Inc. Enzyme Cleaner with Peppermint to the drains each week.
5. Double bag and securely tie each garbage bag. Schedule twice weekly summer garbage removal. Caulk, seal and screen all openings.
6. Spray or sprinkle dry soap or borax into garbage cans or dumpsters after they have been washed (with 1 oz. per quart of Safe Solutions, Inc. Enzyme Cleaner with Peppermint) and allowed to dry; it acts as a repellent. It is best to wash and spray with diluted Safe Solutions, Inc. Enzyme Cleaner with Peppermint first.
7. Place tansy near your kitchen door or where flies tend to cluster. Other repellents include oil of cloves, oil of peppermint or other essential oils and/or mint springs. Try an aroma-therapy machine to dispense these fragrances and repel your fly problems.
8. Set a sponge in a saucer and soak it with oil of lavender to repel flies.
9. A pot of basil set on a window sill or table will help reduce the number of flies in the room.
10. Spray or mist any remaining visible flies with (1 oz. per quart) Safe Solutions, Inc. Enzyme Cleaner with Peppermint.
11. Make and use some fly traps - either containers or imprinted glue traps.
12. Flies and flying ants and other flying insects are attracted to the light, so darken all windows but one, or turn off all lights but one

and/or install one black light or ultraviolet light and then vacuum up those pests that are attracted.

13. Mix 90% honey or molasses (the fermenting kind) and 10% food-grade DE as an excellent fly bait. **Keep any any/all baits away from children, pets and wildlife.**
14. Feeding food-grade (amorphous) DE to animals (cattle, sheep, horses, dogs, swine, goats, emus, etc.) at a rate of 1% - 3% of their feed ration controls internal parasites and prevents fly larvae (maggots) from developing in the excrement (droppings).

If you still have flies, 📖read The Best Control© or The Best Control II© on CD-ROM.

INTELLIGENT CONTROLS FOR LICE

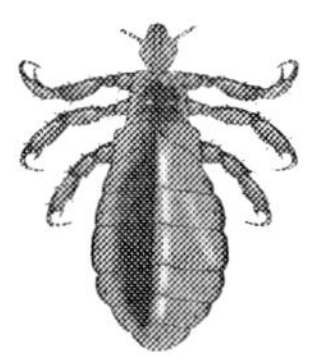

The head louse *(Pediculus humanus capitas)* (DeGeer), the body louse *(Pediculus humanus humanus)* (Linnaeus) and the crab louse *(Pthirus pubis)* (Linnaeus) all occur on humans. All three cause considerable skin irritation as they feed on human blood or crawl on the body. Typhus, impetigo, trench fever and relapsing fever have all been transmitted by body and head lice. Scratching can lead to secondary bacterial infections leaving children feeling achy, feverish and/or lethargic.

Human lice can establish and maintain themselves only on humans. A louse cannot hop or jump. They can, however, crawl fast. They are usually transmitted only through close personal contact. They are less frequently transmitted through the sharing of personal articles or toilet seats. For head lice, this includes combs, brushes and other grooming aids, hats, headbands, helmets, caps, headrests, wigs, curlers or other headgear, especially when these items are stored in shared lockers. They spread or infest by crawling, they live by biting and sucking blood from the scalp and can survive for up to 48 hours off a human head, and the nits on a hair shaft can survive from 4 - 10 days - so vacuum thoroughly and/or spray/clean with diluted Safe Solutions, Inc. Enzyme Cleaner with Peppermint.

Head lice infestations have been a problem a long time - Pliny, a Greek naturalist (23-79 AD) suggested bathing in viper broth. Montezuma paid people to pick nits off his subjects, dried them and then saved them in his treasury. W. Coles in his 1657 book Adam in Eden: or Nature's Paradise noted that the oil from hyssop (Hyssopus) "killeth lice." Nicholas Culpeper in his 1681 The English Physician Enlarged recommended tobacco juice to kill lice on children's heads, a very early reference to the use of tobacco as an insecticide poison. Medical historians trace head lice infestations back 9,000 years! In the U. S. head lice are not "known" to spread disease or cause serious injury - they are only considered to be "repugnant". Like other U. S. public health agencies, the National Center for Disease Control and Prevention have never tracked head lice outbreaks, said official, Tom

Skinner. Sometimes called "mechanized dandruff." Head lice may be nasty, itchy and very contagious, but the pediculicide poisons sold to get rid of lice are even worse.

Important Note: Among the reactions to poison shampoo or lice "treatments" are seizures, mental retardation, many different allergies and respiratory problems, strange tingling, burning, itching, attention deficit disorders, brain tumors, leukemia, cancer and death. **We do not suggest the use of pediculicide poisons to *control* lice.**

1. Thoroughly vacuum each room daily wherever lice have been a problem and spray carpets and floors with (1 oz. per quart) or mop floors with (1 oz. - 2 oz. per gallon) Safe Solutions, Inc. Enzyme Cleaner with Peppermint and/or borax.
2. 🕮 **Read the entire chapter on Lice located @**
   💻 **http://www.getipm.com or**
   💻 **http://www.thebestcontrol.com.**
3. The Author also has used ½ oz. of Safe Solutions, Inc. Lice R Gone® Enzyme Shampoo and/or their Enzyme Cleaner with Peppermint per shampoo-type application to safely remove lice and nits. These non-poisonous enzyme shampoos make the hair so slick lice and nits can't stick and lice can not live off the body for very long. **The natural peppermint in Safe Solutions, Inc. Enzyme Cleaner and in Lice R Gone® repels lice and many other pests.**
4. Be sure each child uses his/her own locker or hook and clothes and hair ornaments, combs and brushes.

Note: Lice are host specific; there are lice that attack goats that will not attack cattle. There are lice that are common external parasites affecting cattle, sheep, goats, swine, poultry and other livestock. Many organic farmers are looking for safe ways to control these pests without using dangerous, synthetic, chemical insecticide poisons. **They should first try a fine-toothed metal lice or flea combs, Not Nice to Lice® or Lice R Gone® or Safe Solutions, Inc. Enzyme Cleaner with Peppermint**. Vigorously shampoo with Not Nice to Lice® enzyme shampoo or mousse per label directions and then, while still wet, comb with a regular comb to detangle the hair and then a fine-toothed metal flea or lice comb should be used to comb 1" sections of hair in order to remove the loosened nits. **Then manually inspect the hair with a bright light for any remaining lice or nits before you rinse.**

There are two kinds of lice that affect cattle/cows: biting lice and sucking lice. Lice are passed between animals as they feed or crowd together. Biting lice move along the topline (spine) and are about the size of a pin head, straw-colored and soft-bodied. Biting lice feed on dead skin and hair follicles. They are very common on cattle, sheep, goats and swine. **All will**

be removed with Safe Solutions, Inc. enzyme cleaners or Lice R Gone® or Not Nice to Lice® shampoos/mousses.

Sucking lice are blue-black and very small; they are attached to the skin. Inspect for them by scraping the skin with a knife and shaking the scrapings onto a stiff piece of white paper. Wash or (better yet) dip each animal from nose to tail with diluted Safe Solutions, Inc. Enzyme Cleaner with Peppermint and borax . Repeat treatment in 2 - 3 weeks. The enzyme/borax wash will still be effective in a dip tank and will control all other ectoparasites. Mix at a rate of 1 quart of Safe Solutions, Inc. Enzyme Cleaner with Peppermint and 5 pounds of borax to 50 gallons of water. (Note: You do not need the borax for lice.)

The word "lice" in Hebrew is "kinim" - one of the plagues God sent to punish Egypt was lice - even to this day parents and farmers respond to lice like they are truly plagues. Exod. 8:16-18

A staggering 20 million Americans find out each year we live in a lousy world - when they become infested or plagued with lice! The really lousy part of this is many are treated repeatedly with dangerous, volatile, synthetic pesticide poisons that no longer control the lice; some people have treated their children 10, 20 and even 30 or more times with over-the-counter poison shampoos without getting rid of the lice!

Enzyme, Surfactant and Peppermint Caution: Some people may experience a moderate skin irritation or slight eye irritation when using a combination of enzymes, surfactants and/or peppermint oils, such as those in Safe Solutions, Inc. Products.

Caution: Before "treating" with any volatile pesticide poison shampoo or lotion, read the Material Safety Data Sheets (MSDS) for not only the active poison ingredient, but also for all of the "inerts." Never apply any pediculicide poison shampoo in the shower. The warm, close environment can allow a dangerously high amount of the poison to be absorbed. Observe all warning labels. Do not use a shower cap. These poisons are especially dangerous for pregnant or nursing women, children younger than 2 months, or anyone with asthma.

If you still want to use the dangerous poison shampoos or pediculicides, you won't get control because many lice are already immune or resistant to these poisons; if you doubt this check out

http://www.vegsource.com/wwwboard/parenting/messages/3581.html.

As an alternative, routinely wash with salt water and start combing - Once lice are detected, plan on spending one full day for each initial treatment, then daily for at least 2 weeks. Give yourself at least an hour per head - and with long hair, as much as two hours per head. Make sure your child is comfortable and occupied. Use an entertaining video, arts and craft project or coloring book to keep your child entertained and engrossed. Use a bright light, magnifying glass and metal (flea/nit) comb. Wash with hair conditioner and comb through each strand from top to bottom, removing nits with fingernails, combs, blunt scissors or tweezers. If the nits will not budge, snip off the hair. **Recheck your child's head every 3 - 4 days for several more weeks.**

Start cleaning - Everything that has been in direct contact with the infected child - bedding, clothing, towels, toys, dolls, cars, furniture, hats, combs, brushes - must either be vacuumed, laundered or dry cleaned daily; any items that can not go through the washer or the dryer or be thoroughly vacuumed should be placed in sealed plastic bags and kept isolated for at least 2 weeks.

The 1997-1998 head lice season had been particularly bad. Even in February, 1998 school nurses and parents were still telling us that children had their head lice "treated" with poisons 10 - 20 or even more times! Some children's parents were using over-the-counter poison treatments virtually daily to "treat" the resistant lice, even though the poison shampoo labels clearly warn people not to use these toxins more than once every 2 weeks! Never use any volatile, synthetic pesticide poison more than twice after it fails the first time! Not Nice to Lice® and Safe Solutions, Inc. Enzyme Cleaner with Peppermint and Lice R Gone® do not contain any registered pesticide poisons and they have safely controlled even pesticide resistant lice. **You can also order any of these products directly from Safe Solutions, Inc. at 1-888-443-8738. If you are still having lice problems, 🕮read the latest chapter from The Best Control II© at 💻 http://www.thebestcontrol.com.**

INTELLIGENT CONTROLS FOR MOSQUITOES

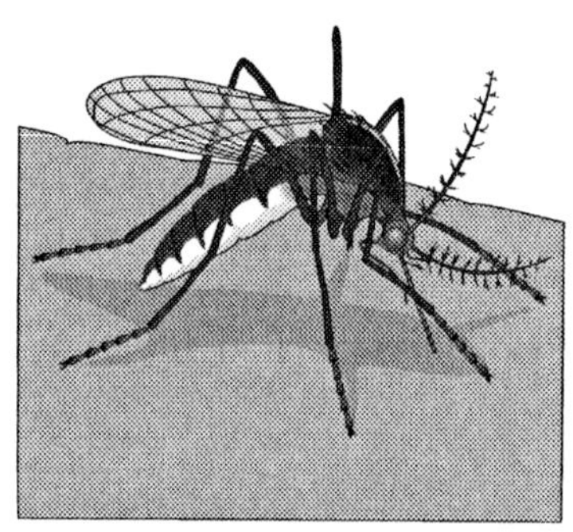

Mosquitoes are blood-feeding ectoparasites of people and animals. The English call mosquitoes "gnats". There are about 100 trillion mosquitoes with at least 3,450 different species in the world. They are found from the tropics to the Arctic regions. All of the families belong to the order Diptera and are related to house flies, gnats and midges. What makes mosquitoes different from all other flies is the presence of a long, piercing mouthpart called a proboscis and the scales on the hind margins and veins of their wings. Morphologically, mosquito males differ from females in that they have feathery antennae, long feathery palps and smaller mouthparts. Mosquitoes develop through complete metamorphosis and have four distinct states: egg, larva or "wriggler", pupa or "tumbler" and adult.

Mosquito eggs can be classified into three groups: 1. eggs laid singly on the still or very slow-moving water surface (Anopheles), with each egg having a series of "floats" along its perimeter; 2. eggs laid in groups forming rafts made by the adult females that float on water surfaces (Culex and Culiseta); and 3. eggs laid singly out of the water in the mud (Aedes and

Psorophora). Mosquito larvae are aquatic; they feed on water mites, water fleas, algae, protozoans and minute organic debris by sweeping the food into their mouths with a pair of feeding brushes.

Mosquito pupae also live in the water. Adult mosquitoes are small, about 1/8" long, with a single pair of membranous wings and are free living. A typical mosquito weights about 2.5 milligrams, or about 20,000 mosquitoes per pound. Females of most species require a human and/or animal blood meal before oviposition, utilizing the protein in blood to produce their eggs and bring them to maturity. There are an estimated 10 trillion mosquitoes produced just in the U. S. each summer with about 170 species. To give you some idea how many 10 trillion is - that amounts to 41,000 mosquitoes for every man, woman and child or enough to fill the entire Grand Canyon! A mosquito's brain is the size of the period at the end of this sentence, yet it has outwitted man's "controls" since the dawn of recorded history! **It still can not find a way to fly into a 3 mph wind, however.**

Mosquitoes seriously harm vast numbers of people worldwide by transmitting pathogenic organisms that cause disease and death, especially in tropical areas. Including Eastern, Western, California and St. Louis encephalitis, heartworm, malaria, yellow fever, dengue and filariasis. Malaria is a constant threat even in the United States where known vectors exist. Malaria, among all insect-borne diseases, has been the most deadly in modern history. During the last century alone it had killed between 100 - 300 million people, mostly babies and small kids and it infects and debilitates hundreds of millions of others each year per WHO! CNN Trivia 2/4/98 noted that 700,000,000 people a year are infected by diseases carried by mosquitoes. In comparison, only 21 million people died in combat in World War I, World War II and the Korean War combined.

Over 60 species of Anopheles mosquitoes are known to be capable of transmitting malaria. Travelers returning from abroad can constantly introduce the causal agents of malaria, which are microscopic protozoa in the genus Plasmodium spp. On average, one person dies every 30 seconds as a result of a little mosquito "bite". In Canada hordes of mosquitoes can actually darken the sky - researchers were bitten about 9,000 times per minute; at that rate they could lose 1/2 their blood in 2 hours and die from blood loss! But our primary reason for controlling mosquitoes usually is only to lessen the annoyance caused by their bites and then only secondarily to reduce the transmission of human and equine viral encephalitis and dog heartworm.

The annoyance caused by mosquito feeding can include the itching, restlessness, loss of sleep and nervous irritation in all people, pets and domestic animals that suffer from their attacks. Mosquitoes do not really "bite", but they penetrate their victim's hide or skin with their proboscis or hollow, flexible snout. The female has a pump in her head which she uses like a turkey baster to suck in your blood. The average meal takes about 1 millionth of a gallon per bite. Their saliva makes us itch. Usually this minor annoyance can not be documented in terms of economic loss, but, obviously, there may be some major economic losses, e.g., decreased recreation income and lower milk and beef production due to blood loss and irritation. Occasionally extremely large numbers of mosquitoes can actually cause the death of domestic animals through blood loss and anaphylactic shock from reactions to mass injections of mosquito saliva.

Mosquitoes are not strong fliers - so fans easily blow them away. The reproductive success of mosquitoes depends in a large part on the ability of gravid females to locate and select oviposition sites that will support the growth development of their offspring. Safe Solutions, Inc. Enzyme Cleaner with Peppermint diluted in water (1 part per 50,000 parts of water) create an adverse environmental condition that renders the water repellent and/or lethal to all stages of growth.

Maintain tight screens and weather-stripping. Use sodium vapor lamps or yellow non-attractive light bulbs at outside entrances. Remove or empty frequently any containers that may hold rainwater (flower pots, tires, cans). Clean out clogged roof gutters holding stagnant water. As a last resort, add light-weight oil to surfaces of ponds, ditches and even animal hoof prints in mud where mosquitoes may breed. Community effort is needed. Try the proper, professional use of entomopathogenic bacteria, e.g., *Bacillus thuringiensis* strains (Bt) or *Bacillus sphaericus* (Neide) (Bs), another important pathogen of mosquitoes, diluted Safe Solutions, Inc. Enzyme Cleaner with Peppermint, dehumidifiers and/or fans and other Intelligent Pest Management® controls before spraying any volatile, synthetic pesticide poisons.

1. Remove all sources of stagnant or standing water if possible, e.g., old tires, bird baths, cans, trash barrels, wading pools, etc., or add Safe Solutions, Inc. Enzyme Cleaner with Peppermint, at a rate of 1/3 oz. per gallon of water.
2. Spray the area and drains with Safe Solutions, Inc. Enzyme Cleaner with Peppermint (1 oz. per quart of water). Remove or spray bushes and dense shrubbery and vines by doors and patios with hose end sprayers and enzymes (1 - 2 oz. per gallon of water).
3. Turn on fans to “blow them away.” Sit in the breeze (even if it is from a fan). They will not bother you.
4. Mosquito bite relief: Soak bites in Epsom salt water or apply a paste of salt mixed into lard or cold cream.
5. Lighting fogging or spraying diluted Safe Solutions, Inc. Enzyme Cleaner with Peppermint (2 oz. per gallon) or garlic oil will control mosquitoes immediately.
6. Rub citronella oil or scented geraniums on clothing or exposed areas or burn citronella candles or wash yourself, your pet and your clothes with Safe Solutions, Inc. Enzyme Cleaner with Peppermint.

7. Pennyroyal, rubbed on the skin (if your are not sensitive), tansy or scented geraniums planted near a door, or basil plants will repel mosquitoes. Wear protective clothing or vinegar on the skin. CNN 8/28/01: Iowa State says catnip is 10x more effect than DEET, so a very small amount of catnip oil can be a very effective mosquito repellant.
8. Practice proper exclusion; repair 16 to 18 mesh screens; seal windows and doors and caulk.
9. Caution - Test anything you want to put on your skin only on a small area first.
10. Some people are more attractive to mosquitoes than others. Mosquitoes are attracted to dark clothing, carbon dioxide and sweat. Prime feeding times are late dusk and early evening. Some people react more seriously to mosquito saliva, the chemical that causes the bites to swell and itch. Carry a small "spritzer" bottle filled with very diluted Safe Solutions, Inc. Enzyme Cleaner with Peppermint, apply and rub into to bite area - this normally will reduce the swelling and itching.

If you still are seeing mosquitoes, 🕮read The Best Control© or The Best Control II© on CD-ROM - ☎Call 1-800-221-6188. Note: The latest chapter is at 💻http://www.thebestcontrol.com.

INTELLIGENT CONTROLS FOR OCCASIONAL INVADERS (BOX ELDER BUGS, ELM BEETLES, ETC.)

1. Maintain routine and thorough sanitation and proper food and garbage storage. Routinely clean and spray with diluted Safe Solutions, Inc. Enzyme Cleaner with Peppermint.
2. Vacuum up all visible pests inside and spray them with (1 oz. per quart) Safe Solutions, Inc. Enzyme Cleaner with Peppermint outside.
3. Steam clean and/or mop the floors with 1 oz. of Safe Solutions, Inc. Enzyme Cleaner with Peppermint and/or ½ cup borax per gallon of hot water. **Don't allow crawling children or pets to contact borax on the floors.**
4. Lightly sprinkle talcum or medicated body powder, baking soda, a little lime, or ground calcium chloride (Comet® or finely ground Tums®) or food-grade DE inside and outside.
5. Be sure to eliminate all moisture and plumbing problems, and reservoirs hiding/breeding areas).
6. Change the exterior lighting to yellow bug lights or sodium vapor lighting (at hardware or farm supply stores).
7. Install and properly maintain vents, air conditioners, dehumidifiers and/or fans.

8. Closely mow grass and eliminate leaf litter, ground cover, general litter, and trim all overhanging or touching branches.
9. Spray infested plants with diluted (Lemon Joy®) dish detergent (1 oz. per quart of water) or diluted Safe Solutions, Inc. Enzyme Cleaner with Peppermint (¼ oz. per gallon of water). **Be sure you will not burn the infested plants with your diluted sprays by spraying on a few leaves first and then waiting several hours to see what happens.**
10. Most insect pests die quickly when sprayed with 1 oz. Lemon Joy® dish soap and 1 teaspoon of oil per quart of water. This is the same "dishwater" Grandmother used to control her pest problems.

If you still are having pest problems, 🕮read The Best Control© or The Best Control II© on CD-ROM.

INTELLIGENT CONTROLS FOR RODENTS

Several human diseases are associated with rodent infestations. Rodents can carry more than 200 human pathogens. Salmonellosis is a serious intestinal disorder that can be transmitted to people who ingest food contaminated by salmonella bacteria in rat urine or feces. Murine typhus, leptospirosis, listeriosis and trichinosis are other rat-transmitted diseases. The tropical rat mite, an external parasite of rats, causes severe itching and skin irritation in people. Rats have occasionally been known to bite sleeping people; these bites can result in an infection known as rat bite fever. Plague bacteria can be transmitted from rats to people through the bite of rat fleas. Over $120 million is spent in the U. S. alone each year on rodent "control" programs.

1. **Sanitation:** Institute good daily cleaning procedures, food storage and garbage removal. Use 1 - 2 oz. per gallon of water Safe Solutions, Inc. Enzyme Cleaner with Peppermint and borax (½ cup per gallon of water) to clean and help remove urine, excrement and food particles in all infested or suspect areas on a routine basis. All fiberglass insulation should be removed from around refrigerator and freezer condens- ers and motors. Keep exterior areas clean, close mown and trimmed. Glue traps should be checked daily and any trapped mice removed and disposed of in a dumpster. Live traps should be checked daily and mice drowned in a pail then disposed of in a dumpster. All trash bags should be removed as soon as possible. Doubled trash bags should be used to prevent leakage. Also, it is important that both of these bags be securely tied shut to prevent leakage into the dumpster. Dumpsters

should be cleaned with diluted Safe Solutions, Inc. Enzyme Cleaner with Peppermint and/or borax (at the above-mentioned rates) twice per month in winter and weekly in summer to remove any food residue. All equipment, floors and walls also need to be routinely sanitized to remove food residue and mouse urine and/or excrement.

2. **Exclusion:** All gaps around plumbing pipes and holes in walls and floors should be repaired or at least plugged with steel wool and/or aerosol foam insulation. Remove all exterior debris.
3. **Eating Areas:** All eating must be in clearly designated areas only so that custodial staff can ensure it is cleaned up.
4. **Food Storage:** It is extremely important that all food (and garbage) be properly stored in heavy duty plastic, glass or metal containers. Items such as noodles, flour and grain products that are open must be stored in these containers to prevent contamination. Storage pallets must be 18+" away from walls so inspections can be made. Please remember that proper sanitation, exclusion and food storage are the key elements to successfully combating any rodent problems. Trapping or baits will not eliminate the reason for the mice being present anywhere.
5. **Set live multiple catch traps or glue boards** baited with a Cheerio or little piece of cookie wherever you see any droppings.
6. **Other Rodents Controls:** Make a "Walk-the-Plank®" trap by putting 7" of water in the bottom of a 5-gallon pail covered with a 3" of floating oats or sunflower seed and a yard stick or board up to the rim. For rats, use a garbage can filled 2/3's with water. Beer, e.g., Bud Light or Pepsi that still has its "fizz," will kill rats and other rodents. (They can not get rid of the gas.) Mice and voles die when fed baits with vitamin D. Dried pea diets sterilize mice.
7. **Repellants:** Peppermint will often repel mice, so routinely clean with Safe Solutions, Inc. Enzyme Cleaner with Peppermint.
8. **Outside** - "Fumigate" active burrows with carbon dioxide or carbon monoxide. (You can use lit charcoal briquettes to create the carbon monoxide. You can use dry ice or a cylinder of CO_2 to create the carbon dioxide.)

9. **If you are still seeing rodents 🕮read <u>The Best Control</u>© or <u>The Best Control II</u>© on CD-ROM. ☎Contact Get Set, Inc. @ 1-616-677-1261 or at 💻<u>http://www.getipm.com</u>.**

Note: Fourteen cents is the rattail bounty for the 1997 rat season in Bangladesh. In 1996, Bangladesh bounty hunters killed 2.6 million rats. Anyone who kills 10,000 rats wins a color television.

INTELLIGENT CONTROLS FOR SCORPIONS

Although many people who live outside the arid southwest United States may never see a live scorpion, its shape is well known, and they can be found as far north as British Columbia. The scorpion's body form is characteristic, cephalothorax (fused head and thorax) elongate and dorsally shield-like, with an abdomen distinctly segmented with the last 5 segments tail-like ending in a stinger usually curved upward. The most common scorpion is the small, striped scorpion, *Centruroides vittatus* (Say) family Buthidae. This small arachnid is only about 1½ inch long, tan, with two broad dark stripes running lengthwise down the body. It is distributed across the southern states and can be commonly found under rocks on south hill slopes in Virginia, Kentucky and Missouri. Non-fatal, poisonous species occur in Florida and in the semi-arid Southwest.

Two species are known to cause fatalities when they sting: *Centruroides gertschi* (Stahnke) and *C. sculpturatus* (Ewing) commonly called the Deadly Sculptured Scorpion or Bark Scorpion. These scorpions are from the family Buthidae are found in southern Arizona and neighboring states of California, New Mexico, and Texas. Actually *C. gertschi* is only a color variation of *C. sculpturatus*. There are about 40 species of scorpions in the U. S. - all of which can sting! Scorpions are most common in rural areas and new subdivisions.

Scorpions are nocturnal. They hide under boards, rocks, rubbish and litter during the day. Scorpions are nocturnal feeders, so they forage at night, detecting slight air movements and/or minute vibrations, seeking insects, and sometimes, small mice. They can normally withstand starvation for 4 - 5 months. Scorpions blindly grab their prey with front, crab-like claws and quickly and repeatedly sting, whipping the stinger over their back. **Scorpions can not see ultraviolet light, but ultraviolet light makes scorpions fluoresce - so, go out at night with a black light and carefully hunt this pest**.

Despite the scorpion's usual occurrence in dry climates, scorpions need access to water, or some moisture. Because they do need to drink water, their nocturnal feeding habits and tendencies to inhabit shady crevices and areas reduce the evaporation or loss of their body fluids. The crevices they hide in may be extended down to the moist areas of the soil.

Scorpions also find daytime hiding places in crawl spaces, attics and closets. They enter occupied rooms, especially kitchens looking for water. Scorpions avoid temperatures over 100° F. and when the attic gets too hot they move downward into the laundry, bathrooms and/or kitchen where water is available. So, make some water traps.

Inspection - Thoroughly soak an area near the foundation with water and diluted Safe Solutions, Inc. Enzyme Cleaner with Peppermint (1 - 2 oz. per gallon of water). Then cover with a piece of OSB board,

plywood, paneling or heavy cardboard with a rock on top - check this "shelter" for several days for scorpions hiding under there and remove them or make a trap of diluted enzyme cleaner or soapy water in a shallow tray under the cover. Conduct a nighttime flashlight (or better still a black light they glow a fluorescent green color) inspection. Place hands carefully when searching in scorpion habitats. Wear high boots, heavy gloves and long sleeved shirts and then:

- Carefully, look under outside harborage and in crawl spaces and attics with a black light at night.
- Scorpions avoid temperatures over 100$_o$ F. and when the attic gets too hot - they simply move downstairs into the laundry, bathroom and/or kitchen areas where moisture is also available.
- Inspect kitchen sink cabinets and bedroom closets.
- Scorpions fluoresce under ultraviolet or black light; (they can not jump) so control is relatively easy.
- Ground scorpions frequently burrow into sandboxes where they can remain without food and water for up to 6 months - you may have to screen the sand to protect the kids.
- Scorpions tend to lie still and blend into their surroundings.
- Shake and examine all clothing and shoes before putting them on.
- Move furniture and beds away from the walls.
- Don't walk in bare feet. Always wear shoes when outdoors, especially around a pool at night or when ever in damp areas.
- Be especially careful of wet/damp towels in the bathroom and pool area.

Habitat Alteration

- Maintain an 18" vegetative free band around the perimeter of the building.
- Tighten, weather-strip and/or caulk all points of entry. They usually enter by way of wall voids, so seal all visible openings. Store firewood, lumber, and garbage up off the ground.
- Remove harborage, e.g., piles of wood, debris and/or trash around buildings and homes.
- Repair plumbing leaks and ventilate moist areas.
- Install screened vents or fans and/or a dehumidifier and/or a non-leaking air conditioner.
- Insects are their principle food, so control the insects and you control the scorpions.

Exclusion and Controls

- Repair door thresholds, door, vent, and window screens, caulk and/or seal all openings.
- Put crib legs in clean wide-mouthed jars, pull beds away from walls, shake all clothing before putting it on - remember, scorpions tend to cling to loose objects.
- Dampen a burlap bag or piece of heavy, coarse cloth and spread it on the ground in the evening. Scorpi- ons will crawl under it during the night and can be easily collected the next morning.
- Use a black light and vacuum dry crawl spaces and attics, as a last resort have caring certified applicators dust under kitchen sinks and in closets where scorpions are seen with desiccating dusts, e.g., food-grade DE or try talcum powder or medicated body powder to baking soda or Comet®.
- Foam/seal/caulk all cracks and crevices and/or voids.
- Chickens will search out and destroy this pest outside. Now, the Mexican government even puts ads on TV advocating chicken control.
- Cats usually of little value in mice control can be quite effective in controlling scorpions, but they must be trained how to do so safely!
- Water baits with boric acid, borax, food-grade DE, diluted Safe Solutions, Inc. Enzyme Cleaner with Peppermint or sodium borate or water/soap traps placed where scorpions can reach them but children, pets and wildlife cannot, will work.
- No commercial baits are available, but you can experiment with the above-mentioned materials.
- In dry places, scorpions will congregate under moist burlap placed on the ground in areas of suspected activity. Carefully inspect and control the moisture seekers.
- Routinely mop with diluted Safe Solutions, Inc. Enzyme Cleaner with Peppermint and/or borax (1 - 2 oz. each per gallon of water.).

PUBLIC HEALTH IMPORTANCE - **Caution: Every scorpion sting should be considered dangerous**. Always consult a medical professional. Children, chemically-sensitive people, people with heart problems and/or elderly people are especially susceptible to the scorpion's poison. **Call a doctor or emergency room immediately and cover with ice or immerse the bitten area in ice cold water**. Scorpions sting when touched, rolled over on when sleeping, stepped on, or otherwise provoked.

Remember that your initial inspection must be done very thoroughly. Some scorpions can live for 6 months without food or water and can hide for months after eating their fill. Carefully look all over - very thoroughly. Scorpions usually breed outside or under the building, possibly in the attic, but in most cases will be found in the crawl space, under logs, timbers, rocks, debris, or similar material. Thoroughly clean and caulk the entire building area so there will be no hiding places left for the scorpions. Thoroughly inspect at least an area for ten feet around the outside of the building and remove all debris, boards, rocks, firewood, etc. If you prepare boric acid or sodium borate water baits and they evaporate - simply add more water to the container - the boron products will still be there waiting to go back into the solution. Do not add any more boron to the bait container unless you first wash it. If you use Safe Solutions, Inc. Enzyme Cleaner with Peppermint as a spray, use it at a rate of 1 - 2 oz. per quart. Note: Chickens love to search out and destroy scorpions.

Inside the building, remember scorpions can and do hide anywhere, so carefully look everywhere in bathtub traps, in seldom worn shoes and boots, in areas under appliances, under sinks, in closets, and in similar dark or damp hiding places. All of these areas can be vacuumed and/or spot treated with lime, talcum powder or medicated body powder or Comet®, boric acid, silica gels and/or diatomaceous earth for effective control. Routinely clean with (1 - 2 oz. per gallon of water) Safe Solutions, Inc. Enzyme Cleaner with Peppermint and/or borax.

Be sure to correct all leaks, routinely and thoroughly vacuum and clean the premises, use dehumidifiers apply silica gels, boric acid, Comet®, lime, talcum powder or medicated body powder lightly in all cracks and crevices, then caulk with silicone all openings. If you must use poison, follow the labeled product directions exactly and vacate the building for at least several days and thoroughly air out before re-entry.

About 300 B.C., Theophrastus, in book 9 of his Enquiry to Plants, noted that wolfsbane, or scorpion plant *(Aconitum anthora)* kills scorpions if it is shredded over them. Pliny in book 20 of his Natural History, written in the first century A.D. advised that a mallow leaf *(Malva)* "placed on a scorpion paralyzes it."

Final Note: Use a black light inside and out. Chickens love to eat them let - let 3 to 4 chickens clean the exterior area for you for real innard-grated pest management. Diluted Safe Solutions, Inc. Enzyme Cleaner with Peppermint and/or borax or, as a last resort, food-grade DE will kill scorpions when directly contacted. Remember, if you live in an infested area, put bed legs in wide mouth jars as scorpions can not climb on clean glass. Beds should not touch walls. Wrap bed legs with duct tape (sticky-side up) and place duct tape (sticky-side up) around walls and where you see scorpions. Do not walk without shoes or at least sandals. Look underneath all objects you pick up and take out: clothes, bedding, footwear before getting into them. Turn on lights when getting out of bed and watch where you step and touch. **Routinely clean, mop, and/or spray with diluted Safe Solutions, Inc. Enzyme Cleaner with Peppermint and/or borax.**

If you still are having problems with scorpions, 🕮read <u>The Best Control</u>© or the <u>Best Control II</u>© on CD-ROM.

INTELLIGENT CONTROLS FOR SPIDERS

Spiders are seldom ignored. Their distinctive appearance, habits, and intricate webs command attention and evoke strong emotions. Given their due, spiders should be prized for their role as predators and natural regulators of insect populations, but because of their appearance and human cultural fears, when one is found to be potentially dangerous, sensationalizing it is irresistible. There are at least 35,000 species worldwide and at least 3,000 spider species and about 40 families in the U. S.; they are all categorized in the class Arachnida, order Araneae. Like their arachnid relatives the mites, spiders live in all parts of the world where they quietly make their way, snaring living prey in their webs or ambushing insect prey in episodes acted out in minute jungles and deserts.

Spiders are a diverse group and are the primary arthropod predators that naturally regulate many insect pests. The two-part spider shape is well known. Its head and thorax are combined to make the cephalothorax. Four legs are attached to each side of the cephalothorax. Spider eyes are in front - some have very large eyes. Like all arachnids, spiders have no antennae or wings and they have 8 legs - insects have 6. They consume up to 2 times their own body weight daily. They live everywhere - some species have been kept alive for over two years without feeding. Population densities of spiders are estimated to range from 27,170 to 5.4 million/ha for some habitats (Bristowe, 1958; Gertsch, 1979).

While all spiders are poisonous to some extent, very few bite humans. Spider mouthparts, located in front below the eyes, have two short needle-tipped appendages, called chelicerae. These needles, or central fangs, are connected internally to poison sacs. The fangs are used to bite prey (mostly other arthropods) and inject poison to immobilize it. Two short leg-like mouthparts help hold their paralyzed prey, while the chelicerae work back and forth tearing the exoskeleton. As blood wells out, it is sucked into the mouth cavity and ingested. Spiders keep working their prey in this way until all the juices are gone and the remainder is a dry crumbled lump. The abdomen is located behind the cephalothorax; it is sac-like, usually globular.

The anal opening is located near the end of the abdomen and close by are some short appendages called the spinnerets. Silk webbing threads out from these spinnerets. Spider silk has great elasticity and can stretch 1/5 of its length without breaking. The silk is protein and is digested by enzyme cleaners that contain protease enzymes. All spiders produce silk, and they use silk in more interesting ways than most other silk producers. Spiders make silk retreats such as tubes and funnels, they make irregular cobwebs as well as the evenly spaced, spiraled great orb webs. Most spiders feed out a dragline wherever they walk and never fall off edges without catching themselves. While spiders don't have wings, they "fly"; nonetheless, by releasing a thread of silk until it is long enough for the wind to catch it and carry them off — the process is known as ballooning. Newly-hatched spiderlings use this method to leave the hatching area. Most species are nocturnal, unobtrusive - often pretending to be dead when molested - most spiders in homes are usually found in undisturbed, dark or dimly lit, cool, damp places - these areas are where people are most likely to be bitten when they "bug", accidentally imprison, or crush these beneficial hunters.

Basically only two spiders are considered dangerous to humans in the United States: the Black Widow and the Brown Recluse. In reality, these two names each represent several different species. Spiders are only distantly related to insects. Unlike insects, they have 4 pairs of legs but lack wings and antennae. Most spiders can be kept out of buildings by tight screens, weather-stripping and caulking. Keep screens and other openings in good repair. Caulk all seams around windows and doors. Indoors: Remove by vacuuming. All spiders are predators feeding primarily on insects and other arthropods but they can survive for very long periods without food. The average spider eats 100 bugs per year. You are never more than 12' from a spider.

Ballooning spiderlings can ascend over 15,000' and have been sighted landing on ships sailing the mid-Pacific. Silk starts as a liquid protein which becomes a solid thread. An orb web may have 1,200 junctions, each crafted perfectly. The spider must calculate the exact length and tension of each succeeding line so the earlier ones don't go slack. Slack lines don't transmit vibrations. The standard orb web is completed in only 20 minutes at about 3 - 4 a.m. Most orb weavers rebuild their webs once a day; they take the web down and eat it to be completely recycled in their body and reused in about 30 minutes. Spiders coat their feet with an oily fluid from their mouths so they don't stick to the webs. Spiders can replace lost legs.

First Aid: For any bite or sting it is important to reduce stress and help the inflicted person to relax. There is evidence that this will reduce the toxic effects of some bites and stings (Ebeling 1975). An ice cube may be applied for a short time to reduce pain at the site of the bite or sting; this does not reduce the effect of the bite, but may make the afflicted person more comfortable. (DO NOT IMMERSE THE WHOLE LIMB IN WATER.) If in doubt about the seriousness of a bite or sting, or if a person is bitten or stung by any of the medically important species discussed in this chapter or book - contact your local poison control center or a physician immediately. Also, collect the spider in question if possible to assist in the treatment of the bite or sting. **Always see a physician if bitten by any spider**.

The bite of most spider species is not considered to be dangerous. But, any bite or sting may elicit an unusual allergic reaction by persons who are hypersensitive to the bite or sting of a specific species. For this reason all bites must be examined to ensure the safety of those involved. A hyperallergic reaction can lead to anaphylactic shock and in very severe cases, respiratory distress may develop. It is not unusual for a person to have some pain and numbness in the same region as the site of the bite. However, if, for instance, a person is bitten on their hand and their legs begin to swell, this is indicative of a systemic reaction, and this person should receive medical attention as soon as possible.

People who are known to be hypersensitive to other stinging insects such as bees and wasps are not necessarily hypersensitive to spider bites. Likewise, each spider has a very specific type of venom and a person may be sensitive to the venom of one species and not sensitive to the venom of a closely-related species. Lastly, some anti-venoms are available for treatment of some bites and stings, but their availability is variable. **Contact your local poison control center for information regarding anti-venoms if dangerous spiders are a problem in your region.**

1. **Inspection** - A thorough inspection of the building is essential and should be made at night because most spiders are nocturnal.
2. **Proper Identification** - Accurate identification is important for both pest management and medical reasons. Place glue boards/monitoring traps or duct tape (placed sticky-side up) in the area where the spider was seen.
3. **Prevention/exclusion** - This consists of making sure that the building is in good physical condition, and properly screened and sealed to reduce entry. Also, changing the exterior lighting to off-building locations, from mercury vapor to sodium vapor lamps or amber lights, or in the case of homes, changing the bulbs near the entrances to yellow bulb, may be of some help in reducing insect/spider attractive-ness. Install vapor barriers, vents, fans, air conditioners, and/or dehumidifiers to change the conditions conducive to infestation.
4. **Sanitation** - Such practices consist of keeping the premises free of debris such as boxes, papers, clothing, scrap and lumber piles, etc.; it is wise to wear protective gloves and clothing when cleaning out such accumulations of clutter. A thorough housecleaning should be done a minimum of twice each year. Try lightly sprinkling talcum or medicated body powders or Comet® around sill boxes and openings. Routinely vacuum and clean with Safe Solutions, Inc Enzyme Cleaner with Peppermint (1 oz. per gallon of water).
5. **Mechanical measures** - The key to control is the timely mechanical removal of all visible spiders, webs, but especially the egg sacs with a vacuum, both inside and outside; seal or wrap the bag in plastic and properly dispose of the bag immediately after you finish vacuuming.
6. **Spray** - 1 oz. of Safe Solutions, Inc Enzyme Cleaner with Peppermint per quart of water will kill most spiders in a few seconds.

7. **Dehumidifiers and Ventilation** - The reduction of moisture reduces many insect infestations which limits spider food sources. Spiders like most arthropods are also very sensitive to moisture loss and will quickly leave overly dry conditions. So properly ventilate and install and maintain fans and/or air conditioners and/or dehumidifiers in basements, crawl spaces and attics.

Follow-up

When webbing is found, either vacuum or sweep it down, which will also eliminate spiders and egg sacs. This will help you determine your degree of control on future visits. Note: 1 acre may contain 2 million spiders. There are about 50 spiders for every square foot of grass. Remove or exclude the insect pests they feed on. Routinely steam clean or thoroughly wash/clean with Safe Solutions, Inc Enzyme Cleaner with Peppermint and/or borax. Remember spiders are beneficial creatures.

1. Vacuum up all visible spiders, webs and/or egg sacs (300 hundred spiders may be in one sac).
2. Routinely clean (with 1 oz. per gallon) or spray (with 1 oz. per quart) of Safe Solutions, Inc Enzyme Cleaner with Peppermint and/or borax. **Borax will kill plants.**
3. Spray straight 5% white distilled vinegar with a teaspoon of coconut oil to help remove and help prevent spider webs.
4. Routinely steam clean or vacuum the entire area. Do not store clothes, packages, materials for extended periods of time without cleaning them all or sealing them in plastic.
5. Lightly sprinkle talcum or medicated body powder or Comet® or food-grade DE in sill boxes and along walls, etc.

If you still are seeing spiders, 🕮read The Best Control© or The Best Control II© on CD-ROM.

INTELLIGENT CONTROLS FOR STINGING INSECTS

The insects considered most beneficial to humans are found in the large insect order Hymenoptera. Not only are the bees and many of their relatives pollinators of flowering plants, including fruits and vegetables, but thousands of species of small wasps are parasites of other arthropods including pest insects. Without these parasites that limit the growth of insect populations, pests would overtake most of our crops. Volatile, synthetic pesticide poisons are not species specific. They kill everything, including all the beneficial insects - and maybe you, your family and pets.

The urban pests of the order Hymenoptera are the stinging insects. Although the first image to come to mind implies danger to humans, these yellow jackets, hornets, and wasps sometimes serve our interest: they feed their young largely on flies, spiders and/or caterpillars. But, in 1990, 32,662 small animals in the U. S. required a trip to the vet after being stung by bees or wasps. In 1988, the Federal Center for Disease Control in Atlanta reported 34 human fatalities due to known wasp or bee stings. About 100,000 U. S. citizens are stung yearly by wasps or bees. The majority of stinging victims suffer normal reactions to the venom, such as pain and swelling. A smaller number of people will be hypersensitive to the venom and can suffer a fatal anaphylactic shock reaction.

Many of these stinging insects are social. They live in colonies with a caste system or a division of labor and overlapping generations - all offspring of one individual reproductive. Some of these colonies persist: foroverlapping generations - all offspring of one individual reproductive. Some of these colonies persist: for many years (ants, honey bees) and others, like stinging wasps, start anew each year.

In parts of the United States, particularly in the eastern states, yellowjackets, wasps, hornets and bees are all called "bees" by the general public. Of course the general public is principally focused on one attribute these insects have in common - their stingers. If stung, try a little fresh squeezed onion juice or a meat tenderizer paste or diluted enzyme cleaner and/or see a doctor.

Knowledge of the behavior of these pests is essential to their management; effective communication with frightened or, at best, fearful occupants is an important skill you must develop. Nests of stinging pests are usually the target for control. Understanding nesting and the make-up of the colony is essential.

How to avoid being stung: Bee-ware!

1. Do not cook or eat or drink outdoors during yellowjacket season.
2. Do not wear light blue, yellow, and/or brightly colored and patterned clothes or bright flashy) jewelry.
3. Do not wear scented talcs, perfumes, colognes and other scents, including scented hair spray, suntan lotion, sunscreen, cosmetics, deodorants and shaving lotions.
4. Do not sit down on or handle wet towels, washcloths or clothes without first checking to make sure no yellowjackets are drinking the moisture.
5. Do not carry sugary or meat snacks in open containers.
6. Do not drink soft drinks from open containers. Use a glass or a lid and/or a straw.

7. Do not hit or swat at bees or yellowjackets. Squashing a yellowjacket can release a chemical pheromone (alarm) that signals other wasps and yellowjackets in the area to come attack you. Yellowjackets will not usually sting or bite a person at rest, if they or their nest have not been disturbed or threatened by a person's swatting or by the quick movement of their arms or legs. They may land on your skin to inspect a smell or even to get water if you are sweating heavily, but they will leave of their own accord if you stay calm and do not move quickly. If you lack the patience, you can brush them off gently with a piece of paper as long as you move slowly and deliberately.
8. Do not walk directly into the flight paths of these stinging insects.
9. Do not go barefoot, especially through vegetation.
10. Do not shine a flashlight or cast a shadow on the nest at night. Use a red light.
11. If a bee or wasp enters your moving car, pull off to the side of the road and stop, if possible; open the windows and safely let it fly out and leave by itself.
12. Wear proper safety protection, not only during treatment/control but also during inspections.
13. Wear gloves when picking up rocks, timbers and firewood. Use a rake to move debris and mulch.
14. Don't vibrate, hit, move, touch or make any unnecessary movements around the nest.
15. Activities, e.g., running, screaming, and flailing only agitates wasps and bees.
16. **Final Note: If you have any sensitivity to insect stings, you should never attempt any control activity. Bee-Careful!**

General Control Notes - Since bees, yellowjackets, hornets and wasps are all considered to be beneficial insects, control should only be done where there is an imminent threat to people or their pets. These insects can (when provoked) inflict a painful, venomous sting and/or bite. Some people are so sensitive to the venom's complex amino acids, proteins and enzymes they develop severe allergic reactions known as anaphylaxis and may even die without an injection of an antidote. Africanized bees (or killer bees) can and do kill normal people during an attack frenzy that can include hundreds of stings. If the killer bees attack, run away in a zig-zag pattern. Remove or cover all garbage, dropped fruit, soft drinks, pet food and other protein and sugar food sources. Routinely clean all dumpsters, garbage cans and spills, then routinely clean or spray with diluted Safe Solutions, Inc. Enzyme Cleaner with Peppermint and/or borax. If you spray stinging insects with 1 oz. per quart of Safe Solutions, Inc. Enzyme Cleaner with Peppermint, they generally die within a few seconds, or simply vacuum them up. Safe

Solutions, Inc. Enzyme Cleaner with Peppermint (1 oz. per quart of water) will kill them all on contact and also has a "fumigant" action.

1. **Wear protective clothing.** Spills and dumpsters should be cleaned up regularly with Safe Solutions, Inc. Enzyme Cleaner with Peppermint and borax. Never caulk an active nest/hole. Plastic barrier tape can be used to cordon off active infestations to protect children from "investigating" the infested area.
2. **Spray any visible stinging insects and nests with Safe Solutions, Inc. Enzyme Cleaner with Peppermint (1 oz. per quart).** Spray paper wasps with soapy water to make them "drown." Use a hose-end sprayer filled with dish soap to flood and remove wasps, hornets, mud daubers and their nests. You can also spray them with rubbing alcohol. Bee careful.
3. **Secure the sucking end of a vacuum by their nest opening at night**. If you use a rinse-and-vac fill it with 3" of soapy water; if you use a dry vac, add 1 teaspoon of talcum powder or 2 tablespoons of cornstarch. If their nest opening is over 1", make it smaller. Turn the vacuum on before dawn and let it run until dark. Repeat as needed. Only after the nest is emptied should you caulk the opening. Duct tape, copper mesh, spackle, caulk, hydraulic cement and screens are exclusion materials that should be used abundantly. **Vacuums can also be used to quickly and safely remove stinging insects from inside the building. Bee careful!**
4. **Make 2-liter wasp traps** by cutting off the top (where the bottle begins to curve up), invert it into the bottle (like a funnel), duct tape the edges, add 2" - 3" of Blue Hawaiian Punch or sweet orange pop (add 1", make it smaller, some hamburger if needed) and set out or hang from trees and facias wherever you see stinging insect activity. You can also make a good bait with a mixture of fruit juice and beer. Once inside the beer gives off its CO_2 which is heavier than air and pushes the air out. The CO_2 in the trap quickly suffocates the stinging insects. You can also use carbonated fruit juice to get the same result. Sticky window fly scoops or fly paper or glue boards in window casings will often catch individual stinging insects as they fly to the light of the window. Turn off all but one light or darken all windows but one and vacuum them up. **Bee careful!**

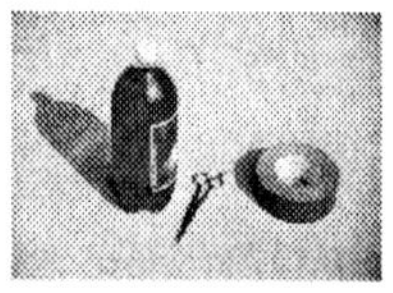 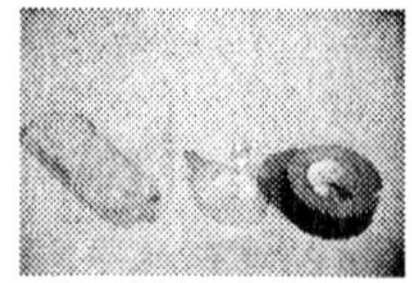 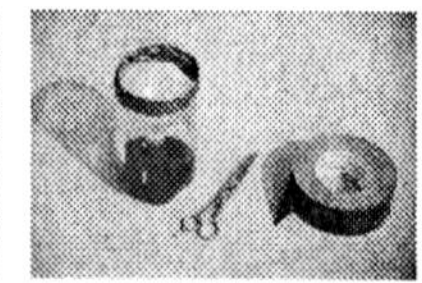 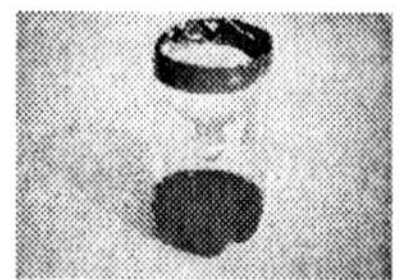

5. **Dust ground nests at night with talcum powder or Comet® or medicated body powder or food- grade DE** and/or soak them thoroughly with diluted Safe Solutions, Inc. Enzyme Cleaner with Pepper- mint (1 - 2 oz. per gallon of water) with a hose-end sprayer at night. Cover them at night with a clear glass bowl or piece of plate glass and leave covered for 2 weeks until they die. You can also "fumigate" ground nests (at night) with 5 lit charcoal briquettes that create carbon monoxide. The carbon monoxide is heavier than air and will kill the underground nest. Bee careful not to get stung or to start a fire! An alternative, safer fumigant is dry ice; the CO_2 is also heavier than air. **Bee careful!**
6. **Rinse empty dumpsters** with a hose then spray diluted Safe Solutions, Inc. Enzyme Cleaner with Peppermint to the point of run off and double bag and securely tie all trash. Install strong fans to literally blow yellowjackets away. Spray the clean dumpster with diluted borax (1-1/2 cup per gallon of hot water). A garbage can with a domed, fitted top with vertical swinging doors will keep yellowjackets away from the garbage.
7. **At night (with a red light)** inject aerosol foam insulation into the entire nest if it is in a tree cavity or in a log or in an exterior wall void.
8. **You can "fumigate" ground nests with carbon dioxide or carbon monoxide.**
9. **Never seal any nest site entrances until you are sure all activity has ceased.**
10. **Make sweet liquid baits with 5% food-grade DE or borax in honey or molasses and place the baits out of reach of children and pets in yellow caps or dishes.**

If you still have stinging insects, 📖read <u>The Best Control</u>© or <u>The Best Control II</u>© on CD-ROM.

Tips for Relieving Insect Bites - There are venom extraction kits now available and commercial sting reliever kits, but nothing works as well as not being stung or bit in the first place.

Try spraying diluted Safe Solutions, Inc. Enzyme Cleaner with Peppermint from a small "spritzer" bottle on the bite as a sting reliever.

To avoid insect bites, avoid wearing perfume, bright colors and flowery print clothes or bright jewelry. People who are highly sensitive should consider immunothereapy (desensitizing procedures) and consult their medical provider about emergency kits.

INTELLIGENT CONTROLS FOR STORED PRODUCT PESTS

About 300 different types of moths, weevils and beetles can be found eating "our" stored food products (grains, peas, beans, spices, nuts, cheese and macaroni mixes, pancake mix, raisins, cereals, pasta, etc.) in "our" pantries, home decorations, animal bedding, dog food, birdseed, dried fruits, candy, etc. Many of these pests are now resistant to commonly used pesticide poisons, but there are some safe and effective ways to prevent and control them.

First, recognize where you have the problem. Look for flying moths or caterpillars in cupboards on walls and ceilings or beetles crawling around near or in food. Look for evidence on and in packages such as pests or tiny holes in strange places, cast-off skins, tracks, fine dust, excrement, etc. Look for and vacuum them up off walls and from behind moldings, pictures, clocks, wallpaper paste, flower pots, hinges, and in cracks and crevices.

The first step and main control is to throw away all pest infested foods and spices. Then install and properly maintain air conditioners, fans and a dehumidifier which will reduce humidity to a point that it is disagreeable to insects. Use 20 mesh screens that fit windows and doors properly.

1. **Routinely and thoroughly clean/vacuum the cupboards and pantry.** Clean the entire area with (1 oz. per gallon) Safe Solutions, Inc. Enzyme Cleaner with Peppermint.
2. **Purchase insect-free products.** Look at the food package very carefully when the box or bag is opened initially and later on. If you buy a new infested product from a store, return them and/or go to another store. **Store all susceptible foods in sealed insect-proof containers or in the refrigerator and/or below 50_{o} F.**
3. All broken containers, torn sacks and spilled foodstuffs and/or infested material should be removed and tossed out promptly. Dispose of all out-of-date and/or infested food stuffs. Lightly sprinkle baking soda or talcum powder. Practice first in/first out inventory control. **Supplies should be properly stored and used as quickly as possible.**
4. Dry animal feed and pet food should be stored away (isolated) from cereal products and dried fruits. Keep it in the freezer if possible, or at least stored in a tightly sealed pail.
5. Store all food stuffs in insect-proof glass containers and/or below 50_{o} F.
6. A good trap for moths is one part molasses with 2 parts of vinegar; place in a yellow bowl. Clean as needed. Lightly sprinkle baking soda or talcum powder or food-grade DE.
7. Install and properly maintain air conditioners, fans and a dehumidifier.

8. Use 20 mesh screens that fit windows and doors properly.
9. Purchase and use stored product pheromone traps at your grocery or hardware store. The odor attracts insects of the opposite sex, similar to how human pheromones affect us.
10. Steam clean with a Vapor Dragon®.
11. Food-grade DE is wonderful for controlling all stored product pests and it is safe enough to eat.

If you still have pantry pests, 🕮read <u>The Best Control</u>© or <u>The Best Control II</u>© on CD-ROM.

INTELLIGENT CONTROLS FOR TERMITES

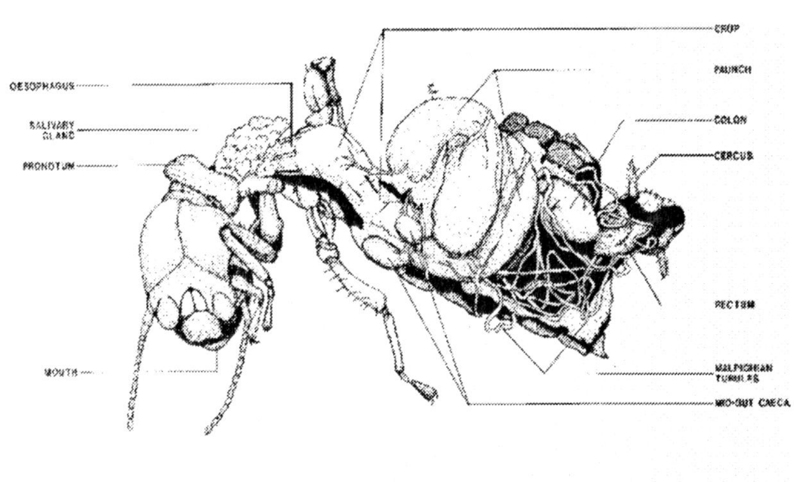

DIGESTIVE SYSTEM OF A TERMITE WORKER (*Zootermopsis nevadensis*)

Far more volatile, synthetic pesticide poison is used to control termites than any other structural pest you will ever encounter. No volatile synthetic residual insecticide or economic poison is completely safe no matter what the professional pest control industry claims. The U. S. Environmental Protection Agency (EPA), when it approves one of the economic poisons, basically is only concerned with the harmful effects that occur from a single exposure of only the active ingredient by any route of entry or its acute toxicity expressed as its LD50 or LC50 value which is the lethal dose or concentration (relative amount) of only the active ingredient required to kill 50% of a test population, e.g., male rats. LD50 values are recorded in milligrams of active ingredient per kilogram of body weight of the test animal. LC50 values are recorded in milligrams of active ingredient per volume of air or water. Both units are the same as parts per million (ppm) which compares to 1 minute in 2 years or 1 inch in 16 miles. Inert ingredients, metabolites, contaminants, synergistic effects and chronic exposures are not evaluated, even if they are more toxic or restricted than the active ingredient.

With the ever increasing and skyrocketing violence, asthma, heart arrhythmias or irregular heartbeats and/or heart attacks, cancer rates, pulmonary problems, health problems, neurological diseases and the rapidly accumulating data that exposes the toxic disruption of our endocrine systems that control all sexual traits, fertility and reproduction, all life as we know it is literally hanging in the balance. That is why we recommend you use mechanical alteration and only sodium borate and refuse to use any volatile, synthetic residual pesticide poisons.

In the 1990s, the EPA listed over 2,518 chemicals that it allows manufacturers to add to pesticide poison formulations as *inert* ingredients. Inerts can include antifreeze, wood alcohol, asbestos, solvents, stabilizers, emulsifiers and preservatives. Many synthetic residual pesticides are 80% to 99% *inert* ingredients. In addition, in some cases EPA allows pesticide poisons to be manufactured using recycled hazardous wastes or to contain contaminates such as DDT or dioxins.

Forty of the *inert* ingredients allowed by EPA in pesticide formulations are also classified by EPA as *inerts* of toxicological concern. This means they are: probably human carcinogens, known animal carcinogens, brain or nervous system toxins, capable of causing other chronic effects or adverse reproductive effects, or acutely toxic at concentrations of one part per million or less to some tested species. Methyl bromide is an extremely toxic fumigant that is easily inhaled or absorbed through the skin. EPA considers methyl bromide so dangerous that it permits only certified pest control applicators to use products which contain it as an active ingredient. However, EPA has also classified methyl bromide as an *inert* ingredient, meaning that the pesticide manufacturers may add it to other pesticide poisons without even testing it or even listing it on the *registered* label! Therefore, the real dangers of these poisons is not currently accessible.

If you are chemically sensitive, we suggest you only try termite predators, e.g., nematodes and/or predator mites, baits, antibiotics, salts, fans, food-grade DE, dehumidifiers, rain gutters, proper grading, ventilation, moisture barriers, sand barriers and/or mechanical alteration, then if you still have any pockets of resistance the only natural chemical/pesticide we recommend that you use is called sodium borate; it is a naturally occurring material that has trace amounts of arsenic; TIM-BOR powder has no added inert ingredients; BORA-CARE liquid also contains ethylene glycol and water; IMPEL RODS are solid borate fungicide rods. If you can not find them, spray all unfinished sole plates, sill boxes and infested wood with 1½ cups of borax per gallon of hot water 3 times to the point or run-off, letting the wood dry between each spraying. In addition, we also recommend you use other non-toxic controls such as exclusion, mechanical alteration, temperature controls, biological controls, sanitation and other integrated pest management techniques. We are firmly committed to your safety and we will always attempt to help you permanently control your pest problems with the least amount of toxin possible! **ALWAYS FOLLOW THE LABEL DIRECTIONS AND REMEMBER BORAX AND/OR BORON PRODUCTS WILL NOT PENETRATE FINISHED WOOD!**

What are the dangers? If you are still thinking about hiring someone to apply hundreds of gallons of some volatile, synthetic *residual* poison in your building - please only have them treat outside and spot treat inside only if absolutely necessary. Be very careful, especially if there is a well within 100' of any soil treatment. Do not let anyone treat your home's interior with any synthetic *residual* termiticides, especially if you have heat ducts in your slab or have a crawl space that is used as a plenum air space or if you have unsealed cracks or expansion joints in your slab floor or foundation, or if your blocks are visually open on top, or if anyone in your home is over 60, under 1, pregnant, chemically sensitive, allergic or has any breathing problems.

It has now been estimated that over 75% of all U. S. homes built prior to April, 1988 are still contaminated with significant levels of chlordane - do you really want more poison contamination? When you compare the typical organophosphate termiticide label with the agricultural label, you find the termite poison label allows the professional to apply over 300 times the amount of active ingredient inside your home than what is considered to be a safe application to an acre of ground outside and yet the same label states it is unsafe and illegal to apply this diluted poison inside a barn where the animals or birds will be used for food!

Remember that before the introduction of any of these synthetic residual economic poisons called termiticides, homes and barns miraculously stood for centuries. It is far more important to protect your health than to try to save a few 2" x 4"s with synthetic poisons that will continue to volatilize into your home for years and years and years!

Volatile, synthetic residual pesticide poisons or termiticide poisons supposedly kill or repel either by poisoning the soil or contacting the insect. This means contamination of nearby water sources and ambient air can occur and/or that toxic surface and ambient air contamination may be present for years after their labeled and "registered" poison application. Sodium borate is applied directly to the wood, thereby eliminating most potential soil, air or water contamination. Sodium borate penetrates throughout the wood and leaves no toxic surface residue. The sodium borate is left as micro-crystals of borate salt inside the wood which will not decompose or volatilize (vaporize) like volatile, synthetic residual pesticide poisons. This means the sodium borate will keep providing you broad spectrum protection (permanently) with little impact on our environment or your health. We suggest that you (re) design and construct your home and additions to minimize moisture uptake and retention by wood; use a dehumidifier; remove all branches that overhang or touch your home; correct all earth-wood contact points; repair all cracks and crevices; thoroughly caulk, screen paint and/or seal your home, and sometimes that you replace your porches, piers and stoops with sodium borate treated and sealed lumber. **Since 1953 when non-volatile sodium borate was mandated in New Zealand to be used to treat and pretreat lumber and homes and buildings, there has never been any evidence of even one successful attack of wood destroying organisms in New Zealand, no matter what the conditions.** Compare this to the failure of toxic and volatile termiticide poisons routinely failing to protect our homes during the same time period and you need go no further with your choice of termiticide - but the poison industry and the regulators ignore little facts like these.

The Environmental Protection Agency (EPA) has officially stated in court that EPA registration (and, therefore, labeled usage) does not assure safety. Current pesticide registration clearly is not designed to protect the public's health; that is why the National Academy of Science (NAS) estimates that 1 out of 7 of us is already significantly impaired by pesticides and other toxic chemicals. The National Cancer Institute studies show children get leukemia 6 - 7 times more often when pesticides are used in or even around their homes, and farmers and pesticide applicators show similar increases in cancer when exposed to these poisons. Drinking water in at least 39 states is already contaminated with these toxins. We clearly are already destroying/poisoning ourselves and the next generations!

The Inspection

A thorough, accurate yearly inspection is the most important part of any wood destroying organism control program and will ensure early detection of infestations and/or reinfestations before serious damage can occur. Before you even begin your inspection, completely read and understand this manual and become knowledgeable in the biology and habits of the various wood destroying organisms so you will know what to look for. Proper termite identification and a knowledge of the species' biology are the most essential elements in termite control. Then carefully and visually inspect all accessible areas, probe and/or sound all accessible structural members and wooden objects inside and outside your home. **Be sure you look under all rocks and patio stones for subterranean termites who may be there looking for moisture and decaying organic matter**. In Florida and the rest of the South (and when baiting) check every 3 months.

Be sure to write down everything you find, i.e., type of infestations, damages, inaccessible areas, conditions conducive to infestation, construction problem(s), moisture problem(s), etc. and carefully record all of this on graph paper as a permanent record. **Written notes, properly recorded and properly filed away, are the only things that do not forget. (Check out the forms available on The Best Control II**©.)

Remember to save and properly file the results of all of your inspections so that you can compare/monitor the conditions conducive to infestation, damages and other details with each passing year. Remember you should conduct a thorough inspection at least once a year and should continue to visually monitor your home as you clean and conduct normal preventative maintenance on it. Remember to make a graph drawing of your home showing the view from above (a plan) and at least one view from the side (an elevation). This will help you find hidden and/or inaccessible areas you might otherwise overlook inside. Make several copies so you can use a fresh graph each time you inspect your home. If you decide to pay a professional to conduct these inspections for you, tell him in the beginning that **whoever you pay to conduct your inspections will not be allowed to perform any treatments**. This should ensure a more honest opinion on his part. Sometimes the professional will pound on the wall and then use a stethoscope (for hearing behind walls), drill holes into your wall and insert fiber-optic viewing scopes (for seeing behind walls) and/or bring in termite-detecting dogs (for smelling behind walls), but nothing beats a "live-in" inspector (you) who carefully and faithfully monitors your own home daily!

Remember, even if you find evidence of an active infestation there is no need to panic and have some professional sell you a job today or lose your home tomorrow! While all wood destroying organisms can do some damage, there always is time to properly and thoroughly plan your control program and often there is no need for any poison control, especially volatile poisons.

Your inspection, if done properly, will allow you to decide how you can best control your wood destroying insect infestations, whether you will use exclusion, mechanical alteration, baits, sodium borate, spot or overall applications, traps, heat or cold treatments, biological controls, salt, dehumidifiers, fans, vents, air conditioning, vapor barriers, medications, Peladow®, borax, Safe Solutions, Inc. with Peppermint or various dusts, alternative borate products, sanitation, or a combination of these or other controls.

A key difference between sodium borate (or borax) and traditional synthetic residual chemical termiticides is that rather than treating the soil or fumigating, sodium borate can be injected, sprayed, fogged or brushed directly on/into bare wood. It penetrates into the wood so that more than just the surface is treated, and because sodium borate does not decompose or change with time, true long-term protection is provided. The product is ideal for wood that is not in contact with the ground and not exposed to rain or excessive standing water. Native subterranean termites are killed with only 1,000 ppm of boron in wood. Formosan termites are killed with 2,000 ppm of boron in wood. Dampwood and drywood termites are killed with 1,000 ppm of boron in wood. Where you have a steady, severe plumbing leak or moisture problem, it should be repaired before sodium borate is applied. Moisture is a key factor in the mode of action of sodium borate. The higher the moisture content of the wood, the faster sodium borate (or borax) diffuses into it and the deeper its penetration. In addition to treating the wood you can also treat sawdust, wood pellets, tongue depressors, scraps of wood, (rolls of) corrugated cardboard etc. with 3% or less sodium borate and use them as baits and/or pre-baits. If you get some on glass, quickly remove the residue with soap and hot water.

1. Vacuum up all termite swarmers. Check all wood with a moisture meter.
2. Soak all the damp and/or infested and/or exposed (unfinished) wood with 1 - 1½ cups borax (and ½ cup Safe Solutions, Inc. Enzyme Cleaner with Peppermint) in 1 gallon of hot water at least 3 times to the point of run-off.
3. Remove all earth/wood contacts, roots and foam board insulation.
4. Install and properly maintain dehumidifiers, vents, fans, eaves and downspouts.
5. Prebait with virgin cardboard wrapped in plastic, but opened at the bottom, moistened with fresh seltzer water that still has its "fizz". Once you have termites in your bait, lightly mist some new cardboard with 3% or less TIM-BOR® or borax or diluted Flagyl®. Shake some termites from the infested station into the treated station and then replace in the ground. Continue to replace with new, treated bait stations as needed. Food-grade DE applied under the slab or on the crawl surface will permanently control termites.

If you still have visible termite activity, 🕮read The Best Control© or The Best Control II© on CD-ROM.

INTELLIGENT CONTROLS FOR TICKS

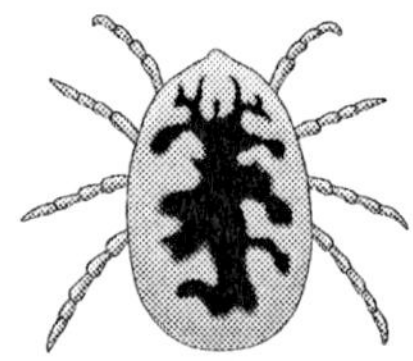

Ticks are not insects; they belong to the class Arachnida, which also includes mites, spiders and scorpions. Ticks differ from insects in that they have one body region, eight legs and no antennae. Ticks are the largest members of the order Acarina and are virtually the only members of that order you can see without magnification. The order Acarina (ticks and mites) to which they belong differ from other arachnids in that their bodies are not conspicuously segmented, but the abdomen and cephalothorax are fused into one body region. They can not fly, run, hop or jump; they climb up and perch on an object until some host passes by; then they either climb on or fall on to the unfortunate creature. They feed entirely on blood of vertebrates with barbed, piercing organs; they take a firm grip on the skin and suck blood for anywhere from 15 minutes to several days - they keep on drinking until they are full.

Ticks are further divided into two families: hard ticks in the family Ixodidae, and soft ticks in the family Argasidae. Hard ticks have a hard, smooth shield on their backs and are tapered at the front with an apparent head; they are the ticks most readily recognized by most people. Female hard ticks feed once and lay as many as 10,000 eggs or more. Soft ticks lack the shield-like plate on their upper surface, have a tough, leathery, pitted skin and no distinguishable head and look like animated pieces of bark or debris. Some soft tick females can feed several times and lay 20 - 50 eggs after each meal. Both groups can swell to considerable size after a blood meal. Ticks have 4 stages in their life cycle: egg, larva, nymph and adult.

Examine all of your pets' and livestock's heads, especially around their ears and necks daily for engorged ticks. Keep vegetation, weeds and brush mowed and closely trimmed. Avoid infested areas. Remember ticks cannot burrow through clothing, so always wear protective long-sleeved shirts and trousers when visiting infested areas; tuck your pant legs into your socks. Closely inspect for ticks on your own or others skin or clothing every few hours. Their favorite places to attach to people are on the legs, thighs and groin, in armpits, along the hairline and in or behind ears.

Don't be modest when inspecting for ticks. Remember the ticks may be very small, so look for new "freckles". Vacuum baseboards and other cracks and crevices thoroughly to remove and destroy eggs and immatures. The best way to remove an attached tick from people or pets is to first apply a dab of menthol shaving cream or alcohol, fingernail polish remover or petroleum jelly before grasping the tick with a pair of tweezers or forceps as close to the head as possible and gently but firmly pull the tick straight off. Do not heat or pinch the tick with your gloved fingers, tweezers or forceps as this may inject the contents of the tick into the wound. Apply an antiseptic to the bite. Save the tick in a small vial of alcohol so it can be identified.

Ticks are of great medical importance because of their ability to act as vectors of five major groups of organisms which cause disease in humans (bacteria, viruses, rickettsiae, spisrochaets and protozoans). Ticks can also cause a condition known as tick paralysis.

If bitten by a tick, seek immediate medical attention.

Ticks are extremely dangerous external parasites of warm-blooded animals, birds, reptiles, amphibians and man. Their bites are not only annoying and painful but may result in localized skin inflammation, secondary infection and possible introduction of disease-causing microorganisms or pathogens. Some ticks are venomous and produce very painful bites and some ticks cause tick paralysis and lameness in people and animals. Both males and females feed on blood. Male ticks generally die shortly after mating.

Because tick movements and bites are seldom felt, you must carefully and frequently examine for ticks on your own body and clothing. Early tick removal is important since many disease organisms are not transferred until the tick has fed for 2 - 8 hours. **More than 65 disease-causing pathogens are now known to be transmitted by ticks, making this group of parasites one of the most dangerous from the perspective of human and domestic animal health.**

To control ticks on pets:

- Inspect at least daily. Wash routinely with Safe Solutions, Inc. Enzyme Cleaner with Peppermint if pets are found frequently infested, try using some food-grade DE rubbed into their coats. Dogs should be protected with volatile pesticide products only if they roam freely in tick habitat. Do not touch treated pets. An alternative is to wash your pet with Not Nice to Fleas®, or with water and natural soap, or 1 - 2 oz. Safe Solutions, Inc. Enzyme Cleaner with Peppermint per gallon of water and/or you can use a herbal rinse - put 2 pounds of fresh or dried rosemary in a ½ pint of boiling water, steep for 20 - 25 minutes, strain, allow to cool and rinse your pet with the cooled liquid - do not towel off, simply allow to air dry or use a hair dryer. Be sure your pets are dry before letting them outside. Try using menthol as a personal and/or pet tick repellent. As a last resort, carefully rub 5 - 10 drops of rose geranium essential oil diluted in 1 tablespoon of almond oil or food-grade diatomaceous earth into their fur per label directions.
- Advise that all uncontrolled or ownerless dogs be regulated and/or impounded.
- Use of flea and tick collars not only have variable results but also can be dangerous to people and pets.
- Cats do not currently appear to be at risk from Lyme disease nor are they hosts for RMSF vectors.
- Keep pets within your own mowed areas.

To control ticks in yards and buildings:

- Lightly dust with food-grade DE and place duct tape (sticky-side up) wherever you suspect ticks as this should help control ticks in buildings.
- Lightly dust or grid your yard with 2" wide strips of food-grade DE.

The Author has used Safe Solutions, Inc. Enzyme Cleaner with Peppermint to spray ticks and/or ot wash pets with ticks. Ticks die in about 2 minutes when exposed to this product.

If you still are having tick problems, 🕮read the appropriate chapter in <u>The Best Control</u>© or <u>The Best Control II</u>© on CD-ROM.

INTELLIGENT CONTROLS FOR MOLDS - FUNGI

Mold is one type of fungi which include yeasts, mildews and molds. All fungi require external food sources and normally high moisture levels to develop. Allergies can cost up to $2 billion yearly in medical costs, prescriptions and decreased productivity - up to 10 million work days are missed each year and every day allergies keep 10,000 kids out of school!

The number of allergy sufferers has soared in the last 20 years as more and more contaminants fill the air, water and food. High levels of mold and/or fungi, e.g., *Aspergillus versicolor* can create many health problems, especially if a person has allergies; symptoms can be itching, eye irritation, vomiting, diarrhea, breathing problems, a sore throat, runny nose, headaches, congestion, and even life-threatening collapse from anaphylaxis. *Stachybotrys chartarum* (or *atra*) is a greenish-black mold that can grow on high cellulose mateirals with low nitrogen content. It needs constant high moisture to survive. This mold can cause nasal congestion, fever and eye irritation.

Sometimes volatile organic compounds (VOC's) are created and residents can really get sick. At every school where we have had them mist the area and clean the ducts with diluted Safe Solutions, Inc. Enzyme Cleaner with Peppermint at 1 oz. per quart and mop with and clean all surfaces and ducts with 1 oz. per gallon and/or rinse-and-vac with 2 oz. per gallon, we have controlled the allergy symptoms for at least 30 days with only Safe Solutions, Inc. Enzyme Cleaner with Peppermint. Routine cleaning with Safe Solutions, Inc. Enzyme Cleaner with Peppermint and/or borax or baking soda should quickly control or eliminate any and all fungi and mold problems, especially if you repair all leaking roofs, walls, plumbing and other moisture problems.

Dry out basements and bathrooms/showers - prime breeding areas for fungal spores. Don't use humidifiers, or if you must, only use them with 1/3 oz. of diluted enzyme cleaner per gallon of water. Properly install and maintain dehumidifiers. Circulate air in bathrooms with exhaust fans. Install and maintain (activated charcoal) filters in all ducts in central air conditioning and heating systems. Treat all wet wood and/or cellulose materials you want to save with TIM-BOR® per label directions and mop all floors, etc. with Mop-Up® per label directions or, if you do not have access to these products, use 1½ cups of borax or even 1 cup of baking soda per gallon of hot water; be careful not to put any boron product where it can be ingested. To quickly bring the allergic reactions down, simply mist or spray the room with Safe Solutions, Inc. Enzyme Cleaner with Peppermint enzymes and then install the activated charcoal filters on both sides of a box window fan; then turn the fan on and filter the air...or you can buy a high-efficiency air cleaner. Replace the filters as needed. **Clean routinely with diluted Safe Solutions, Inc. Enzyme Cleaner with Peppermint and/or baking soda or borax.**

1. 5% vinegar will kill 82% of all molds.
2. Sodium borate, borax, salt and lime will kill all mold, but they also may kill plants.
3. Zinc strips and/or bare copper wires have been used to help control mold.
4. Baking soda, food-grade DE and diluted enzyme cleaner will all kill mold. After applying you can help by gently brushing or sweeping the molds away.
5. The proper use of dehumidifiers, vents, fans and/or air conditioners can greatly reduce the amount of mold problems you may have.
6. As a last resort, use 1 cup of bleach per gallon of water to temporarily control mold.

If you still are having mold, mildew or fungi problems, 🕮 read the appropriate chapter in <u>The Best Control</u>© or <u>The Best Control II</u>© on CD-ROM.

SAFE LAWN AND OUTSIDE PEST MANAGEMENT

Weeds basically only grow where grass will not. The poison sprayers say they will "control" pest problems like dandelions, yet every year these "controlled pests" are back in the very same place. Because of all the synthetic pesticide poisons and fertilizers, our top layer of soil is virtually dead. Plants do not chelate well without microorganisms. Soil must be alive, teaming with microorganisms or the lawn and/or plants will not be healthy. Pests like grubs multiply in these dead areas; add organic fertilizer and they quickly disappear. Proper irrigation will control crabgrass. In a few years even the weeds are choked out by healthy grass.

Poisons do not protect; they kill. Before there were any "professional" lawn or pest control operators, we had natural fields full of grass that fed vast herds of buffalo who trampled it with their sharp hooves, yet it always grew strong and tall. This grass was never aerated or irrigated, never fertilized, never had insecticides applied, never had fumigants applied, never had herbicides applied...the grass did extremely well without any man's help. Today we have spent hundreds of millions of dollars to develop grass so weak we must nurse it with fertilizer and poisons many times each growing season and we must constantly irrigate and keep off it or it will die.

The Author brags he has never done anything to his "lawn" but mow it and it stays green all season. You can drive on it and not kill it. You decide if you want a strong, natural lawn that feeds microorganisms and plants and other creatures and is healthy for your family and easy on your pocketbook or an expensive, sick lawn that needs your constant attention and money and may even be harming you.

The EPA estimates that one out of every 10 public drinking water wells in the U. S. contains pesticides, as well as more than 440,000 rural private wells. At a minimum, over 1,300,000 people drink water contaminated with one or more of these dangerous poisons!

Pesticide poisons have been found in thousands of lakes, rivers, and waterways throughout the nation. Agriculture is the number-one source of surface water pollution in the U. S.

In June, 1993, the National Academy of Sciences (NAS) released its long-awaited report on the health hazards posed to infants and young children from exposure to pesticide poisons in the food supply. The Academy stated that any pesticide poisons are harmful to the environment and are known or suspected to be toxic to humans. They can produce a wide range of adverse effects on human health that include acute neurologic toxicity, cancer, reproductive dysfunction, and possible dysfunction of the immune and endocrine systems. Among the NAS's critical findings, existing pesticide poison policies do not protect the young adequately, instead the policies are treating kids as "little adults." Unique dietary patterns are ignored, although they result in far greater exposure to multiple pesticide poisons in food, by body weight, than occur in the adult population. The NAS expressed particular concern over children's dietary exposure to neurotoxic pesticide poisons stating that children tend to retain a greater portion of a given dose of certain toxins than adults and are not as capable of detoxifying them in their bodies. They are at greater risk from neurotoxins since the nervous system in an infant or young child has not yet developed fully.

Cause and Effect - We will never know if what we suspect about toxins having an adverse effect on our health is true - at least not from a purely "scientific point-of-view" - because, we will never be allowed to spray poisons on some statistical group of people (compared with an equal number of unsprayed people) to show actual or direct cause and effect. Because we can not spray people - the polluters of our world can continue to state pollution warnings are only based on *junk science* and only made by chemophobics and that there is no scientific proof that their "registered" poisons pollute, kill, harm or damage our world, people and/or pets.

Rachel Carson studied the failed governmental attempts to prevent the Japanese beetle from reaching Iroquois County, Illinois by repeatedly bombing with volatile, synthetic pesticide poisons from the air in the mid-1950's. Many insect species became sick (or died) from the poison, and were easy prey for insect eating birds and mammals. These creatures then became poisoned in turn and, in ever-widening circles of death, went on to sicken and kill those who fed on their flesh, leaving a landscape devoid of animal life, from pheasants to barnyard cats. The protracted poison war against the targeted pest, the Japanese beetle, on the other hand accomplished nothing; the "pest" continued its westward advance. The planes had been bombing with dieldrin which did remain to contaminate the soil and water for decades to come, like land mines left behind by a retreating army, guaranteeing further ecological tragedies, like the mute testimony of Iroquois County's dead ground squirrels: found with their mouths full of dirt, they had gnashed at the poisoned soil as they died in agony.

Steve House, a friend of the Author, who was personally poisoned by these synthetic pesticide poisons, also saw tree squirrels die, the same way, in his native Detroit after they bombed with volatile poisons there.

Remember, whatever poison is used on your lawn or in your neighborhood will volatilize or be blown into the air by lawn mowers so you breathe it into your lungs. It will touch and enter your skin. It will sink into the soil so it will eventually end up in the ground water or water that comes out your kitchen faucet. Your children will track the lawn chemicals into your home on their shoes and then walk, play and eat on the carpets and floor. Your children will also play ball on the lawn, get the poisons on their hands and then eat a sandwich, so it ends up inside the digestive tract.

In addition, if they put pesticide poisons around the outside of your home around the edges, as a pest "barrier" and spray volatile poisons into the cracks and openings below and around your house, they can easily contaminate the inside of your home. If volatile poisons were ever used in the past by a previous owner, you might still be in danger. If volatile poisons were required by some state laws to be incorporated into the soil under the cement foundation of homes and under slab floors, these toxic vapors can continue to hurt your family for years. These volatile termite poisons definitely volatilize (leak out) into your air and can remain potentially dangerous for generations.

Pest Management at the Crossroads (1997), Consumers Union, Yonkers, NY noted that more than 500 insects, 170 weeds and 150 plant diseases are now resistant to one or more pesticide poisons - just another reason not to use them. True Integrated Pest Management is the fitting together of all pertinent data, constant monitoring and re-inspecting, methods, and common sense to safely control a pest problem. Methods including Pestisafes™, natural enemies, e.g., pathogens, parasites and predators, cultural practices, mechanical alteration, microbial agents, genetic manipulation, exclusion, pheromones, traps, growth inhibitors, temperature controls and even (non- volatile) pesticides which all become mutually augmentative instead of individually operative.

The Journal of the National Cancer Institute, 71(1), July 1983 noted A study of 3,827 Florida pesticide applicators employed for 20 or more years found they had nearly 3 times the risk for developing lung cancer. The same study also showed the pesticide applicators had twice the risk for brain cancer. There was not any increased cancer risk when applicators were studied for only 5 years, implying it takes over 5 years to accumulate enough chronic damage to the genetic structure to develop the cancers.

Children who live in homes where *registered,* volatile, indoor or outdoor volatile pesticide poisons are used face a far greater chance of developing leukemia (leukemia is a cancer of the blood). The study, published in July's 1987 issue of the *Journal of the national Cancer Institute,* studied 123 Los Angeles children with leukemia and 123 children with the malignancy. The results showed the children living in the *registered* pesticide poison treated homes had nearly a 4-times-greater risk of developing the disease. If the children lived in homes were *registered* pesticide poisons were used in the garden as well, the risk of developing leukemia was 6.5 times greater! All of the children in the study were 10 years of age or younger. **Thus proving to some of us with working brains that cancer rates are not increasing merely because we are living longer!**

The *registered* lawn pesticide poison active ingredients, mancozeb and chlorothalonil (used by commercial lawn spray companies as fungicides), have been classified by EPA as *probable* cancer-causing chemicals in humans as they have been found to cause cancer in animals (*Newsweek, May 16, pg. 77, 1988)*). Mancozeb has also been found to react with sunlight to form a new compound EPA categorizes as a *known* carcinogen (*Newsweek, May 16, pg. 77, 1988*). The common lawn pesticide 2,4-D has been shown to increase the risk of lymphatic cancer in farmers 6 times the normal rate according to a National Cancer Institute report (*Science News, September 13, 1986*).

A book from the Office of Technology Assessment entitled, Neurotoxicity: Identifying and Controlling Poisons of the Nervous System noted that an estimated 300,000 farm workers are poisoned by pesticide poisons in the U. S. Studies demonstrate that in addition to acute poisoning, pesticide poisons can cause long-term (chronic) damage to the nervous system.

Groups of test animals exposed to different pesticide poisons used in agriculture and lawn care showed over 50% more hyperactivity following a single exposure to the chemical. One of the main goals of this experiment, conducted by Dr. J. A. Mitchell and colleagues at the University of Michigan, was to investigate activity behavioral changes in test animals (male Swiss mice) following a single exposure to one of 4 different dosages of weed killers and fungicide poisons. The chemicals used included Lasso (containing alachlor), Basalin (containing fluchloralin), Premiere (containing dinoseb) and the fungicide poison Maneb-80 (80% Maneb). Test dosages ranged from a very low .4mg/kg to 4 mg/kg to 40 mg/kg. Even the largest dose was still below the LD_{50} for the animals (the amount needed to kill 50% of the test animals). According to the researchers, the herbicide poisons and fungicide poisons have received few reports investigating their toxicity while their yearly growth and production have grown far more than the insecticide poisons.

The detection of hyperactivity was measured by placing the test animals in steel cages that were equipped with electronic motion detectors which used infrared beams to count specific movements by the animals. After the single chemical exposure, activity was measured for a 4-hour period. Results showed the *registered* weed killer Lasso did not show any effects at the very low .4 mg/kg level, but did show over a 65% increase in activity at the low 4 mg/kg and a 75% increase at the higher 40 mg/kg level. The *registered* weed killer dinoseb also showed no activity increases at the lowest .4 mg/kg dose, but did show a 15% increase at the 4 mg/kg level, and a 54% increase that the larger 40 mg/kg level. Other researchers have reported that activity provides a sensitive measure for evaluating the behavioral effects of the *registered* pyrethroid pesticide poison, deltamethrin, at doses that did not cause the characteristic neurotoxicological syndrome.

In conclusion the researchers stated, "The results of this study suggest that at least some *registered* herbicide poisons, in addition to pyrethrins, organophosphate and carbamate pesticide poisons, can produce behavioral manifestations following accidental exposure ... The effects of the pesticide poisons on activity also support the hypothesis that these agents may affect the central nervous system" per *Neutrotoxicology and Teratology, Vol. 11:45-50, 1989.*

The article, "Chronic Neurological Sequelae to Organophosphate Poisoning. Am. J. Pub. Health Vol. 84, March 1994 noted: ...that pesticide poisoning can lead to poor performance on tests involving intellectual functioning, motor skills and memory.

The pesticide MCPA, used as an ingredient in some lawn pesticides, has been found to damage a part of the brain known as the *blood brain barrier* per *Toxicology and Applied Pharmacology, 65:23, 1982.* The blood brain barrier is the brain's primary defense system which works to keep toxic substances out of the brain cells and is literally protecting all of us from developing immediate neurological illness. The blood brain barrier has been found to be defective more often in patients with Alzheimer's and some psychiatric disorders per *British Journal of Psychiatry, 141.273, 1982.* In fact, the lack of functioning of the blood brain barrier in the human infant has been reported on many occasions as being the reason why an infant is being found to develop brain damage after exposure to common chemicals, while an adult with a mature blood brain barrier does not. Unfortunately, EPA neurotoxicologist Dr. Bill Sette stated EPA **still** does not yet require chemical companies to test any of their pesticide poisons for causing blood brain barrier damage. Another study of 56 men exposed to *registered* organophosphate pesticide poisons detected memory problems and difficulty in maintaining alertness and focusing attention per *Annual Reviews in Public Health, 7:461, 1986.*

The Tulane-Xavier Center for Bioenvironmental Research in New Orleans said that combining two substances common to *registered* pesticide poisons produces a synergistic impact on hormones 1,000 times stronger than the poisons alone. EPA only checks the active ingredient of a pesticide poison; it totally ignores the synergistic effect of two active ingredients, or even the active poison ingredient'(s) interaction with all of the *inerts*. This is like testing only the *active* ingredient in a cake (yeast) - thus, the "product" does not cause cholesterol problems, weight problems, diabetic problems, tooth decay, hyperactivity, etc.. First of all, a pesticide poison does not contain just the ***REGISTERED* ACTIVE INGREDIENT,** which by definition is the poison actually used to kill or destroy a living organism. Pesticide poisons *normally* also contain unregistered ***inert*** ingredients as well as transformation products, synergists, contaminates and impurities, and quite often the pesticide poison breaks down into other materials, known as metabolites, which can even be more deadly than the original poison. Unregistered *inert* ingredients are also often more dangerous than the *registered* active ingredient, although the *law* allows the formulator to keep these untested and unevaluated chemicals secret from you and your doctor, because they supposedly are not added to the poison formulation specifically designed to kill (the pest). *Inerts* make up the majority of the concentrate/formulation and may include xylene, toluene, benzene, or even DDT! How can you honestly or legally *register* a poison label for use of the active ingredient when the *inerts'* MSDS is far more restrictive in allowable usage?

On October 1, 1996, the California Department of Pesticide Regulation (DPR) suspended 21 pesticide products that contain the *registered* fungicide poison, chloreneb, the wood preservative creosote, and unregistered aromatic petroleum distillates, which are commonly used as *inerts* in insecticide poisons. On January 10, 1997 PANUPS announced that Monsanto agreed to change its advertising for glyphosate-based products, including the herbicide Roundup®. According to the State, the Monsanto ads implied the risks of products such as Roundup® are the same as those of the *registered* active ingredient, glyphosate, and do not take into consideration the possible risks associated with all of the unregistered product's *inert* ingredients.

The survival of the human species depends on the ability of males and females to reproduce successfully. Reproduction is a complex process involving multiple stages of vulnerability for parents prior to conception and birth of their offspring. Few established risks factors have been identified for failures that occur during many of these reproductive stages. In industrialized countries, about 1 of every 5 couples experiences difficulty reproducing. National Academy of Sciences Press, 1989. Exposures of pregnant females to a variety of foreign substances may pose a threat to the health of offspring. In addition, exposures of males and females to foreign substances prior to conception can affect both their ability to conceive and the health of their offspring. Reproductive Toxicology 1992; 6:289-292. Timing of exposure to such substances may be more critical than the total dose rate in determining a broad array of outcomes. Environmental Health Perspective 1997; 105:70-77.

In 1994 the EPA noted the U. S. used approximately 1.2 billion pounds of just the pesticides' active ingredients; agriculture used about 939 million pounds (77%), industrial, commercial and government applications accounted for 150 million pounds (12%) and home and garden applications used about 133 million pounds (11%). These figures do not include chlorine, wood preservatives or specialty biocides. World pesticide use was estimated to be 5.7 billion pounds of only the active ingredients in 1995. In 2001, the National Coalition Against the Misuse of Pesticides noted we now use/misuse 4.5 billion pounds of pesticide poisons per year in just the USA!

In 1996 EPA **began** a study to determine how much pesticide (poison) active ingredient residue (contamination) we can *safely* consume - (if we are lucky) we *may* get the results of how dangerous the food we are eating **today** is by the year 2006! When we set up interim numbers for *acceptable* levels of poison in people and pets, we are not only being very arrogant but very ignorant. **This is truly "junk science" at its *finest.***

Urge any neighbors who use poisons or hire "professional" lawn care to read this book. We simply must stop polluting our precious planet. Our children are our most valuable and vulnerable asset, but everyone and every living thing is in jeopardy from the ongoing poison pollution including our pets, birds, fish and other wildlife.

THE BEST LAWN CARE

Pests in lawns and in homes must be approached in a manner similar to medical illnesses. The answer is not a more effective drug for a disease or another deadly poison for a bug. The challenge is to find the cause of a medical or pest problem and then to eliminate it. Then you have nothing left to routinely "treat". This is simply the best and most logical approach. Intelligent or Integrated Pest Management (IPM) is unquestionably the most cost effective and safest way to control pests inside and outside buildings As a healthy lifestyle prevents most illnesses, preventative pest control prevents most pest problems.

THE KEY IS SIMPLE: Find out why you have pests. If you can find and eliminate the cause of the pest infestation, there will be no pests, inside or outside your home. My Mother first taught me IPM when I was about five years old; she said, "Stephen, if you shut the door the flies will not come in." If you simply wash your garbage cans every week in the summer you will kill or prevent 1,000 flies and 2,000 maggots.

SAFE LAWN CARE OR IPM

There are many safe ways to care for your lawn. If you have healthy organic soil with lots of microorganisms you probably will not have any pest or disease problems. If you are going to hire someone, call and find out if

all or **part** of a so called "natural" lawn company's care is truly safe (pesticide free) and if they guarantee to restore the life of the soil. Ask exactly what they use? Ask for MSDS sheets.

INTELLIGENT CONTROLS FOR WEEDS

1. Adjust mower to remove all dandelion heads and collect all clippings that are diseased or infected.
2. Spray weeds in cracks and along fences with straight urea, or 90% urea and 10% Safe Solutions, Inc. Enzyme Cleaner with Peppermint, or 80% urea and 20% ammonia and a sticker, e.g., 1 oz. dish soap or straight vinegar and/or diluted salt or borax or with 3% essential oils or dust them with baking soda or spray with undiluted Coca-Cola. Always do this on a hot, sunny day, as this will help kill the weeds.
3. Cover weeds with black plastic for several days.
4. Start a good organic soil program. **Do not use human sewage.** Use properly composted, organic chicken manure.
5. Put down a fabric (weed control) ground cloth or black plastic with drainage holes in it and mulch or stone over it.
6. Buy a cane flamer that uses propane to wilt weeds.
7. Spread Dow Flake® on areas where you want no plants to grow.

If you still have weed problems, 🕮read <u>The Best Control</u>© or <u>The Best Control II</u>© on CD-ROM.

INTELLIGENT CONTROLS FOR PLANT PESTS

Garden Insects

1. Get a 2-liter plastic bottle, string, one banana peel, 1 cup sugar, and 1 cup strong vinegar. Slice banana peel into strips and insert them into the plastic bottle. In a separate container, combine sugar and vinegar. Pour this mixture into the bottle, then fill it to within two inches of the neck with water. Tie the string around the neck of the bottle, then tie the other end around the lower branches of a tree. Fruit and black flies, yellow jackets, and other insects find the

fermenting banana, sugar, and vinegar more attractive than the fruit on the tree. Once they fly in, they get caught in the sticky mixture and drown. This reportedly works so well that it can make spraying fruit trees with Safe Solutions, Inc. Enzyme Cleaner with Peppermint (1 oz. per gallon of water) unnecessary.

2. Mix 1 cup of liquid dish soap and one cup vegetable oil. Add 1-2 teaspoons of this mixture with one cup of water and spray it on plants.
3. Spray with diluted (½ oz. per gallon) Safe Solutions, Inc. Enzyme Cleaner with Peppermint as needed. Test spray a few leaves before spraying the entire plant.
4. Take an empty spray bottle and fill about 3/4 of the way with water, then add a few drops Ivory® liquid soap, some hot peppers or hot pepper sauce and some garlic. This spray works well, but needs to be reapplied after every storm and/or every couple of weeks.
5. Grind together three hot peppers, three large onions, and at least one whole clove of garlic. Cover mash with water and place in a covered container. Let container stand overnight. Strain mixture through cheesecloth or a fine strainer and add enough water to make a gallon of spray.
6. Mix one tablespoon of a mild dish washing detergent plus one teaspoon of a vegetable cooking oil with one quart of water. This can be safely sprayed on most plants. Remember to spray both the top and the underside of the leaves. You can also add one teaspoon (rounded) of baking soda if you have fungus problems or use diluted apple cider vinegar or a little lime. Food-grade DE will control plant pests.

CAUTION: Make sure any treatment will not burn plants by first spraying a few leaves and then waiting several hours to see the effect, if any.

House Plant Pests

7. Spray with dishwater or 1 tablespoon of soap, 1 teaspoon of vegetable oil and 1 quart of water.
8. Make a spray of garlic, onion, cayenne pepper and dish soap.
9. Spray with 1 rounded teaspoon of baking soda and/or (½ oz. per gallon) Safe Solutions, Inc. Enzyme Cleaner with Peppermint if fungus develops.

Caution: Before spraying anything on your plants, always test spray a few leaves first to see if the spray mix will hurt them.

IF YOU STILL HAVE CONTINUING OR OTHER INSECT OR RODENT PESTS, PURCHASE AND 🕮READ <u>THE BEST CONTROL</u>© or <u>THE</u>

BEST CONTROL II©. ☎CALL 1-800-221-6188 FOR A CD-ROM EDITION OR HOW TO ORDER AT 💻http://www.safe2use.com.

☎Call Safe Solutions, Inc. @ 1-888-443-8738 or 1-616-677-2850 to order Safe Solutions, Inc. Enzyme Cleaner with (or without) Peppermint, food-grade DE, and/or Not Nice to Lice® Shampoo or order from 💻http://www.safe2use.com.

Stephen L. Tvedten, the Author, has field tested Safe Solutions, Inc. Enzyme Cleaner with (and without) Peppermint and has found that at a rate of 1 oz. per quart of water this patented cleaner quickly and safely controls even resistant lice, ticks, fleas, roaches, spiders, ants, insects, mites, fungus, mildew and mold. Aphids and spider mites can be controlled at a rate of only 1 part enzyme cleaner to 500 parts of water. The secret is in the naturally occurring protease enzymes, peppermint and various GRAS surfactants the Safe Solutions, Inc. Enzyme Cleaner with Peppermint contains.

An insectivore plant will literally digest the insects it traps with enzymes. Spiders inject enzymes to predigest their prey and every molting insect uses enzymes to create a chemical "zipper" so it can open and slip of its exoskeleton. When Safe Solutions, Inc. Enzyme Cleaner with Peppermint is sprayed even on resistant insects, they literally melt. There simply is no way for insects to become immune or resistant to enzymes, surfactants and oils. It is the perfect Pestisafe™. In addition, virtually every fungus and mold is consumed - remember the old laundry soap ads with enzymes that had a pac man-like creature eating stains? Well, Safe Solutions, Inc. enzymes not only eat stains, dirt, etc., they also "eat" insects and odors, athlete's foot and ear fungi, bacteria, viruses, ear mites, plant diseases, ticks, fleas, lice and nit glue, ringworm, planters warts, etc. The Author has seen Safe Solutions, Inc. Enzyme Cleaner with Peppermint help wounds heal quickly and found the enzymes quickly give relief to skin infecting rashes and irritations from burns, bites, stings, poison ivy and the like. The Author has also used Safe Solutions, Inc. Enzyme Cleaner with Peppermint as an insect repellent.

The Author has found that 1 oz. of Safe Solutions, Inc. Enzyme Cleaner with Peppermint in a quart of water will control any insect or arachnid pest within a few seconds. Safe Solutions, Inc. Enzyme Cleaner with Peppermint will often give up to 4 weeks residual control for many, many pests. Food-grade DE will kill insects and fungus by dehydration and the Author eats a teaspoonful every day.

In addition, Stephen Tvedten, the Author, who is chemically sensitive, has replaced virtually every cleaner in his home and now only uses various dilutions of Safe Solutions, Inc. Enzyme Cleaner with or without Peppermint to shower with, mop with, shave with, wash his clothes, clean floors, walls and carpets, wash windows, clean roofs and siding, clean his pets, brush his teeth and shampoo using only this wonderful product - the only caution the Author has to make is do not put Safe Solutions, Inc. Enzyme Cleaner with Peppermint into your eyes - like the enzyme cleaners for contact lenses, these materials can burn the eyelids and the debris and materials they clean off your hair should not be put in your eyes. Some people may be more sensitive to the peppermint and should read the MSDS and lab tests found at http://www.safesolutionsinc.com.

CAUTION: If you try any of these alternative controls, we still want you to test them first on a small area of skin to see if you or your family react to them and then test a small area that you want to treat, wash, clean or spray to see if they cause your plants to burn or to make stains and/or cause any sensitivity. Many times using even less product in your water will give you virtually identical pest control, so always try less before you spray more. The first rule is to always do any control as safely as possible. Don't rush! Plan your attack so nothing is hurt but the pest. Think before you act.

HOW TO FIND OUT MORE ABOUT CONTAMINATION AND THE DANGERS OF "REGISTERED" PESTICIDE USE/MISUSE

The EDF's chemical scorecard at http://www.scorecard.org lets you know what polluters are dumping in your area and how a community ranks in terms of pollution.

The following internet web sites have volumes of free information on pesticides:

http://www.pesticideinfo.org
http://www.afn.org/~accpta/pesticides.htm
http://www.nrdc.org/nrdc/nrdcpro/ocar/chap5.html
http://www.ncamp.org
http://www.epa.gov/pesticides/carlist/table.htm
http://pmep.cce.cornell.edu/issues/nas-report-nrdc.html

http:/msds.pcc.cornell.edu/msdssrch.asp
http://www.edf.org
http://www.rachel.org
http://www.sciencenews.org
http://ace.orst.edu/info/extoxnet/
http://www.chemfinder.com
http://www.ewg.org
http://www.wwf.org
http://www.igc.org/pesticides/
http://www.efn.org/~ncap
http://ciin.org
http://www.chem-tox.com
http://www.msdsonline.com
http://toxnet.nlm.nih.gov/
http://www.lawnandlandscape.com/msds

Go to http://infoventures.com/e-hlth/organge/phd93.html to access Review of the Literature on Herbicides, including Phenoxy Herbicides and Associated dioxins - Herbicides and Associated dioxins Volume XXIII: Analysis of Recent Literature on Health Effects. Last modified on: Friday, October 18, 1996 10:47:02. Copyright 1994-1999, Information Ventures, Inc.

U. S. Environmental Protection Agency, Office of Pesticide Programs (OPP), Fact Sheets on New Active Ingredients. Contains comprehensive information on conventional pesticide active ingredients, including year of initial registration, chemical family. U. S. producer, application sites, types of formulations, methods of application, application rates and toxicological characteristics. Fiscal years 1998 and 1999 are available.

OPP will expand this page to include more new active ingredients, as well as those registered in previous years.
http://www.epa.gov/opprd001/factsheets/

Status of Pesticides in Registration, Reregistration and Special Review, 1998 U. S. Environmental Protection Agency. Provides status of pesticides that are undergoing or have completed pesticide registration or review process as mandated by Federal Insecticide, Fungicide and Rodenticide Act. Lists "new" pesticide active ingredients, those initially registered since November 1, 1984, which by law are not subject to reregistration. Available at http://www.epa.gov/pesticides. 458 pp. For hard copies contact National Center for Environmental Publications and Information (EPA/NCEPI), P. O. Box 42419, Cincinnati, OH 45242-2419, phone: 1-800-490-9198; fax: 1-513-489-8695.

Office of Pesticide Programs - Biopesticides and Pollution Prevention Division (BPPD) http://www.epa.gov/pesticides/biopesticides/

The BPPD is responsible for the regulation of all biopesticides in the Unites States. This web site includes a definition of biopesticides, regulatory activity, active ingredients, Federal Register notices, press releases, publications and a related Internet resources section. The regulatory activities section breaks down biopesticides regulations by all types including active ingredient approvals, tolerance applications, and experimental use applications. Fact sheets are also available from the home page.

Pesticide National Synthesis Project
http://ca.water.usgs.gov/pnsp/

The Pesticide National Synthesis Project is part of the U. S. Geological Survey's National Water Quality Assessment Program (NAWQA). The project's objective is the long-term assessment of the status of and trends in the quality of the Nation's water resources. The web site includes a project overview; national summaries and data concerning pesticides in water; special topics, such as contaminants in fish hormones; national maps of pesticide use, and on-line publications from the NAWQA Pesticide Studies Program. The web site includes a search feature, pesticide-related links and a National Map of the NAWQA Study Units.

Virginia Tech Pesticide Programs, Pesticide Site Locator
http://www.vtpp.ext.vt.edu:8080/catlist.html

The Virginia Tech Pesticide Program offers this extensive database of pesticide-related internet resources. Select a source or topic area, like Government Information Sources, Organizations and Educational Institutions, Pesticide News and Newsletters, and Pest Control Product Manufacturers and Other Commercial Sites, to choose from hundreds of possible resources. This database is fully searchable by keyword or subject. Visit, too, the Virginia Tech Pesticide Program web site, available at http://www.vtpp.ext.vt.edu/. This site serves as a clearinghouse for technical information on pesticides and other toxic chemicals. Find information on pesticide education and training programs, pesticide safety teaching resources, and surveys of pesticide use in Virginia.

Pest Management Regulatory Agency (PMRA)
http://www.hc-sc.gc.ca/pmra-arla/

The Pest Management Regulatory Agency (PMRA) is a Canadian government regulatory agency which "protects human health and environment by minimizing risks associated with pest control products while enabling access to pest management tools." The web site is available in English and French and includes contact information for pesticide programs, regulatory information, international activities information, sustainable pest management data, online publications, related links and a headlines section.

Greenbook.net
http://www.greenbook.net/

This site, offered by the Chemical and Pharmaceutical (C&P) press, provides access to the free and subscription-based reference services of their online Crop Protection Reference Manual. The free service provides the most current versions of product labels and Material Safety Data Sheets (MSDSs) available to C&P Press. Documents can be located by brand and company name. In addition to the product labels and MSDSs, a subscription allows access to a single source of product summaries (including all sites and pests on which the product is registered, EPA registration information, restricted use information, common name, etc.), worker protection information, DOT shipping information, and SARA Title III reporting information. A one-month free trial of this subscription service is available.

Version 2.0 of the PAN Pesticide Database is now available at http://www.pesticideinfo.org
The PAN Pesticide Database is the largest and most comprehensive online collection of pesticide data in the world, providing detailed information (at no cost to the user) for about 5,400 pesticide active ingredients, breakdown products, and related chemicals. The database also contains information on more than 100,000 formulated pesticide products (current and historic registrations) from the U.S. Environmental Protection Agency (EPA). Where available, the database provides information on toxicity, regulatory status, aquatic ecotoxicity, and general identification information, including an extensive list of synonyms. Comprehensive documentation defines terms used and cites the sources of the information, along with its currency, accuracy, and comprehensiveness.

The NIOSH Pocket Guide to Chemical Hazards and Other Databases on CD-ROM put out by the US DHHS, Public Health Services, Centers for Disease Control and Prevention, National Institute for Occupational Safety and Health:

It is listed as DHHS (NIOSH) Publication No. 2000-130 of July 2000 (may have been updated since) and is both Windows and Mac compatible. It contains the following databases:

Immediately Dangerous to Life and Health Concentrations
International Chemical Safety Cards
NIOSH Certified Equipment List
NIOSH Manual of Analytical Methods
NIOSH Pocket Guide to Chemical Hazards
OSHA Sampling and Analytical Methods
Recommendations for Chemical Protective Clothing
Specific Medical Tests Publishes for OSHA Regulated Substances

Toxicologic Review of Selected Chemicals
2000 Emergency Response Guidebook.

You can get it by phoning 1.800.35NIOSH or at http://www.cdc.gov/niosh/

Recognition and Management of Pesticide Poisoning - 540988001 (208 pgs.) Call 1-703-305-7666 or 1-800-490-9198 to order from the Certification and Worker Protection Branch of the EPA, Office of Pesticide Programs. or view the publication directly on the EPA site:
http://www.epa.gov/pesticides/safety/healthcare/handbook/handbook.htmepa

ENVIRONMENTAL JUSTICE DATA NOW ONLINE

NEW YORK, New York, April 19, 2001 (ENS) - Different degrees of environmental burden felt by different racial, ethnic and income groups are now documented and available for every community in the U.S., Environmental Defense announced Wednesday.

The information is available free on the group's Scorecard website, http://www.Scorecard.org, which lets users type in their zip codes to get the local facts.

"This access to comparative data in a single place is an important breakthrough for the environmental justice movement," said Gerald Torres, a law professor at the University of Texas and former U.S. Justice Department official. "For the public at large, it will make it possible to see differentials in environmental burdens in our society, not just where those problems are already obvious but place by place throughout the country."

Torres is coauthor, with Professor Lani Guinier, of a forthcoming book on race and politics from the Harvard University Press.

"Environmental justice is important, sensitive, and hard to measure," said Environmental Defense senior attorney David Roe. "We are putting the best measurement data we can find out into public view, so people can see a local picture no matter where they live."

The new service, available in English and Spanish, represents the first time that local level environmental data have been analyzed across the country to show the differences experienced by several different demographic groups, such as people of color and low income families.

"These are first cut data only," Roe cautioned. "The best numbers available today are very far from being perfect measures of the environmental burdens that different people experience - and of course, numbers can't tell the whole environmental justice story. But systematic data on the 'where' and 'how much' of unequal environmental conditions, even if imperfect, will help focus attention and set priorities in this critical area of public policy."

http://chemdef.apgea.army.mil/textbook/Ch-8.pdf - This website has long term effects of chemical agents. If you scroll down to the organophosphates section you will find the long term effects associated with them.

The resource book Hazardous Chemicals in Human and Environmental Health will be available from 6/15/01 onwards as an electronic version free of charge at the IPCS website, http://www.who.int/pcs. The file is full-text html and can be printed. International Programme on Chemical Safety.

The natural Resources Defense Council has launched a website devoted to environmental contaminants in breast milk. It can be accessed at: http://www.nrdc.org/breastmilk/

The Rachel Carson Council, Basic Guide to Pesticides, is now available at: http://members.aol.com/rccouncil/ourpage/samples.htm .

NEW resources on-line at PAN UK
Reducing pesticide hazards in developing countries

A widely-praised series of publications on ***Control of Pesticides and Integrated Pest Management (IPM): Implementation of Farmer Participatory IPM and Better Chemical Management*** is now available on-line (www.pan-uk.org/internat/intindex.htm). PAN *UK* developed the material to guide policy makers in governments and development agencies, and others concerned about pesticides. The materials include:

Progressive Pest Management: Controlling pesticides and implementing IPM (24pp). A booklet recommending a strategy on: establishing control of pesticides; reducing use, risks and dependency on pesticides; and taking action for IPM.

Pest Management Notes a series of short (4-page) briefings, which will be periodically supplemented, now includes:

1. Pest management a new approach
2. Integrated Pest Management
3. Disposal of obsolete pesticides
4. Desert locust control in Africa
5. Prior Informed Consent
6. International chemical initiatives
7. Pesticide procurement
8. Pesticide residues in food
9. Growing coffee with IPM
10. Success with cotton IPM

Guide to Active Ingredient Hazards This tabulated guide to over 1,000 active ingredients provides a quick reference point for chemical names, types, uses, acute toxicity (WHO classification), the Acceptable Daily Intake, reproductive and chronic effects, endocrine disrupting pesticides, environmental effects, national regulation, inclusion in the PIC Conventions known evaluations.

Resource guide to pest management topics, agencies, web sites and databases (32pp). Topics provides a quick guide to commonly-used terms. Agencies lists major international bodies, NGOs, research institutes, industry contacts. Computer resources offers fully updated web-links and on-line databases.

Country profiles: the state of IPM and chemical management in Africa (34pp), provides an overview and information on selected African countries. The profiles include details (current to 1999) of projects which contain a strong element of participatory IPM.

Information will be added to and up-dated periodically.

This material was produced with the support of, and for use by, the European Commission.

THE WHO RECOMMENDED CLASSIFICATION OF PESTICIDES BY HAZARD AND GUIDELINES TO

The top 10 "AgChem Companies" by 1998 pesticide sales in U. S. millions:

Aventis	$4,676
Novartis	$4,152
Monsanto	$4,032
DuPont	$3,156
AstraZeneca	$2,897
Bayer	$2,273
American Home Products	$2,194
Dow	$2,132
BASF	$1,945
Makhteshim-Agan	$ 801

Source: Rural Advancement Foundation International

Environmental Health Information Service - http://ehis.niehs.nih.gov/

"Learn About Chemicals Around Your House" is an interactive web site see: http://www.epa.gov/opptintr/kids/hometour/index.htm designed to teach children and parents about household products, including pesticides, that may contain harmful chemicals. The web site includes information about toxic substances stored in different rooms in the house and answers commonly asked questions on safe use and storage of these products. The site also contains educational games, and tells children what to do if an accident occurs.

A second resource is called "Read the Label First! Protect Your Kids," which is a brochure that provides information on preventing children from being exposed to pesticides and household cleaners by reading and following product label instructions and precautions, keeping products in their original containers and storing products out of the reach of children. This document is available online at: http://www.epa.gov/opptintr/labeling/rtlf/kids.pdf.

"Ten Tips to Protect Children from Pesticide and Lead Poisonings Around the Home" is a brochure that provides simple steps to protect children from pesticide and lead poisonings around the home, and is available in both English and Spanish. This document is available at: http://www.epa.gov/oppfead1/cb/10_tips/.

"Pesticides and Child Safety" is a fact sheet that provides current household pesticide-related poisonings/exposure statistics from the American Association of Poison Control Centers, as well as recommendations for preventing poisonings and first aid guidelines. This document is available at:
http://epa.gov/pesticides/citizens/childsaf.htm.

"Help! It's A Roach" is a roach prevention activity book for kids and parents. It teaches families what they can do to prevent and control roaches without using pesticides. An interactive web site is also available at: http://www.epa.gov/opp00001/kids/roaches/english/.

Some of these resources are also available by calling 1-800-490-9198. More information on Poison Prevention Week is also available at the Poison Prevention Week Council's web site at: http://www.poisonprevention.org/.

Note on Resistance: When I was in the pesticide application business, I noted we usually got about a good year of "control" with every new synthetic pesticide; then we had to move on to the next toxin.

DETOXIFICATION - FOUR WAYS TO HELP DETOX.

1. Simple Detox Formula - Jan Morales, D. O. has found a simple way to detox without sitting in a sauna for hours: Put one tablespoon of (cold pressed) sunflower oil under your tongue for 20 minutes. Swish the oil around while holding it in your mouth. Spit the oil out after 20 minutes into the toilet. Brush your teeth with half baking soda, half salt to get the oil out. Do this on an empty stomach. The procedure can be done 1 - 3 times per day. Quite often this simple procedure will remove intense headaches - virtually immediately.

2. ORGANIC CORIANDER CHELATION PESTO

4 cloves	garlic
1/3 cup	Brazil nuts (selenium)
1/3 cup	sunflower seeds (cysteine)
1/3 cup	pumpkin seeds (zinc, magnesium)

2 cups	packed fresh coriander (cilantro, Chinese parsley) (vitamin A)
2/3 cup	flaxseed oil
4 tablespoons	lemon juice (vitamin C)
2 teaspoons	dulse powder liquid aminos (Bragg's)

Process the coriander and flaxseed oil in a blender until the coriander is chopped. Add the garlic, nuts and seeds, dulse and lemon juice and mix until the mixture is finely blended into a paste. Add a squirt of Bragg's to taste and blend again. Store in dark glass jars if possible. It freezes well, so you can purchase coriander in season and fill enough jars to last through the year.

Coriander has been proven to chelate toxic metals from our bodies in a relatively short period of time. Combined with the benefits of the other ingredients, this recipe is reportedly a powerful tissue cleanser. Two teaspoons of this pesto daily for three weeks is purportedly enough to increase the urinary excretion of mercury, lead and aluminum, thus effectively removing these toxic metals from our bodies. You can consider doing this cleanse for three weeks at least once a year. It is delicious on toast, baked potatoes and pasta.

3. Read L. Ron Hubbard's book entitled, Clean Body, Clear Mind that explains how to detoxify using a sauna and a proper vitamin protocol.

4. Not Nice to Toxins® is a nutritional supplement formulated to aid in detoxification and the removal of toxins and parasites. It is available from Safe2Use, 1-800-931-9916 or Safe Solutions, 1-888-443-8738.

When will "they" get the message?

Politicians and school superintendents may finally get the message when they realize that if a child is sick from poisons or had to stay home because of lice the day they take the census they have lost approximately $6,500 for the year - if they will not protect the children, may be they will protect their pocketbooks and/or assets!

May be farmers will get the message when they read that Cornell University entomologist, David Pimental and his colleagues calculated that $520 million in annual crop losses are caused by pesticide reduction of natural enemies just in the U. S. "Nature Wars" people vs. pests by Mark L. Winston noted insecticide use in Indonesian rice production in the early 1980's destroyed natural enemies of the brown plant hopper and the populations of this pest exploded. The Food and Agricultural Organization (FAO) estimated that $1.5 billion in rice production was lost in just two years. Fortunately, Indonesian President Suharto followed the advice of his specialists and ordered severe reduction in pesticide use, which allowed the natural enemies to increase and brought the pest levels back down below economically tolerable thresholds. When they stopped using "registered" pesticides they finally got pest control. Duh,..........!

The solution? = Call 1-616-677-1261.

FINAL NOTATIONS

When pesticide manufacturers are threatened with the loss of an insecticide/poison, they "work" with the USDA to find a solution acceptable to USDA. The May/June 2000 issue of Ag Retailer noted on page 6 that the EPA requires developmental neurotoxicity studies on Reldan insecticide/poison. Dow Agro Sciences had requested a minor-use exemption to waive these studies. Gustafson LLC, Plano, TX, who markets Reldon, is now working to find a compromise. It is too bad there simply is no precautionary principle involved in the "registration" of economic poisons.

Rotenone - The Washington Post noted on 11/6/00: The organic pesticide rotenone can produce an illness in rats that closely resembles Parkinson's disease in humans, and can selectively damage the specialized brain cells that die in that disorder. About 1 million Americans suffer from Parkinson's disease.

Asthma - The incidence rates for Asthma are rising, according to the U.S. Centers for Disease Control - the number of asthma cases in the United States has more than doubled in the past two decades from 6.8 million in 1980 to more than 15 million today - resulting in 7.4% of all children ages 5-14 having diagnosed asthma. Since "asthma" is not a normal condition, and since the incidence is rising, we must assume there are unexplained factors present which are increasing its incidence.

Our lungs inhale an enormous quantity of particles daily, yet are still able to function properly in most people. All of us inhale a wide variety of particles daily - from car exhaust particles to dust mites - to animal dander - to plastic synthetic carpet fibers - to synthetic pesticide poisons. It is amazing our lungs can even function. However, thanks to our lung's enormous power to cleanse itself via coughing - sneezing and mucous secretions - they can keep doing their job of taking oxygen out of the air and putting it into our blood. There is, however, an ally to the lungs which is much under appreciated. It is called an alveolar macrophage and is a microscopic immune system cell that waits in the wings of your lungs looking for intruders. When an intruder comes on site - macrophages extend long arms around the intruder preventing it from interfering with the alveoli's job and proceeds to digest it. However, researchers at the Department of Immunology, University of Arkansas (Agents & Actions, Volume 37:140-146, 1992) found that when test animals were exposed to chlordane pesticide vapors (found in high levels in many U.S. homes today, then the macrophages become paralyzed in their ability to destroy cancer cells for 24 hours.

Asthma has been found to occur immediately following chemical exposure. Called Occupational Asthma, this medical condition shows first hand what serious harm can occur to a person's delicate lung structure after working in a chemical environment.

Pyrethrum late-breaking news: EPA has recently determined that pyrethrum is considered a probable carcinogen. That is another reason why the Author does not recommend its use.

Pesticide, suicide or homicide, they all kill.—S.L.T.

Note: Life threatening bacteria, e.g., *Shigella, Salmonella, Listeria* and *Escherichia coli* that cause food poisoning, thrive on about 1/3 of the pesticides that Canadian researchers tested. The bacteria grew fastest on chlorothalonil, linuron, permethrin and chlorpyrifos. *(New Scientist,* Oct. 7, 2000, No. 2259, pg. 20, by A. Coghlan, "Food Poisoning Bugs Thrive in Crop Sprays")

Pesticide Poison Note: PANUPS estimated in November 2000 that: "Each year approximately three million people are poisoned and 200,000 die from pesticide use."

Final Note: Steve Tvedten has developed a detox formula that helps to detoxify people and also helps control internal parasites; it is called Not Nice to Toxins®.

NOTE: This booklet has been condensed from The Best Control II. For a list of references write Stephen L. Tvedten.

Want to reach a poison control center anywhere in the U.S.A.? There is now a new single toll free telephone number; it is 1-800-222-1222.

Table 6.3

Caution: Poison manufacturers' labels and/or their MSDS revisions for only the active ingredients may supersede these warnings.

TRADE NAME	COMMON NAME	PRECAUTIONARY/HAZARD STMT.
Avert PT310	Abamectin	5,7,13,15,16,17,18,21,28,29,35, 36,37
Avert Gel	Abamectin	5,7,13,15,16,17,18,21,28,29, 35,36,37
Baygon Bait	Methylethox	1,3,15,15a,17,19,27,31,35,42
BP-100, etc.	Pyrethrins	5,7,14,15,15a,15b,16,17,19, 24,32,34,35,36,39
BP-300, etc.	Pyrethrins	5,7,24,15,15a,15b,16,17,19, 24,32,34,35,36,39
Borid	Boric Acid	3,10,13.19,21,35,36,45
CB-38	Pyrethrins	1,3,14,15,16,18,24,27,35
Contrac	Bromadiolone	1,2,15,17,19,23,28,35,40,41
Cynoff EC WP	Cypermethrin	5,9,12a,14,15,16,17,18,19,32,39
Demand	Lamda-cyhalothrin	1,6,12c,14,15,16,18,19,31, 32,33,35
Demon TC	Cypermethrin	1,2,10,12b,12c,14,15,15a, 15b,17,18,29,32,35,44
Dual Choice	Sulfluramid	17,18,23,31,35
Dursban TC	Chlorpyrifos	2,8,12a,12d,13a,14,15,15a, 15b, 17,18,27,33,35,45
Eaton AC90	Chlorophacinone	2,17,19,35,40,41
Ficam D	Bendiocarb	5,13,15,16,17,18,19,28,29,34, 35,36,37,38
Flee	Permethrin	5,14,15,17,18,19,22,29,32,35, 36,39,44,45

PRECAUTONARY STATEMENTS

1. Harmful if absorbed through the skin.
2. Harmful or fatal if swallowed.
3. Harmful if swallowed.
4. May be harmful if swallowed.
5. Harmful if swallowed, inhaled or absorbed through the skin.
6. Avoid eye contact.
7. May cause eye irritation.
8. Causes substantial but temporary eye injury
9. Causes moderate eye irritation.
10. Causes eye irritation.
11. May cause eye injury.
12. May be absorbed through the skin.
    - 12a May cause skin irritation.
    - 12b Causes skin irritation.
    - 12c May cause allergic skin reactions
    - 12d Excessive absorption through the skin may be fatal.
13. Do not breathe dust.
    - 13a Handle concentrate in ventilated area.
14. Avoid breathing vapor or spray mist.
15. Do not allow to contact skin, eyes or clothing.
    - 15a Wear protective clothing and chemically resistant gloves when handling.
    - 15b Wear eye protection.
16. If contact occurs, wash skin with soap and warm water or eyes with clean water.
17. Wash hands and exposed skin before eating, drinking or smoking and after handling.
18. Wash all contaminated clothing thoroughly before reuse.
19. Keep out of reach of children.
20. Causes irreversible eye damage.
21. Do not apply where children or domestic animals are likely to come in frequent contact with treated areas.
22. Do not permit children or pets to contact treated surfaces until spray has dried completely.

Gentrol	Hydroprene	5,10,12a,14,15,16,17,18,19,45
Maxforce Roach Bait	Hydramethylnon	3,19,23
Precor	Methoprene	1,6,12a,14,15,16,19,33,35
Precor 2000	Methoprene	5,7,14,15,17,22,39
Premise	Imidacloprid	2,5,6,12,12a,13,14,16,17,18,19,22,-33,36
PT270 Dursban	Chlorpyrifos	5,7,12a,14,15,17,19,35,36,46
PT3-6-10 Aero-cide	Trichlorethane	7,12a,14,17,18,24
PT515 Wasp Freeze	Phenothrin	5,7,12a,14,17,18
Recruit	Hexaflumuron	7,12,12a,16,33,35
Siege	Hydramethylnon	4,7,15,16,17,19,31,35,36
Tempo 20WP	Cyfluthrin	5,8,9,14,15,15b,16,17,18,19,22, 23,29,31,33,35,39
Tim-Bor	Disodium Octaborate Tetrahydrate	3,6,17,35,36,46
Torus 2E	Fenoxycarb	5,11,14,15,17,18,20,33,35

23. Do not allow children or pets to play with the baits.
24. Cover or remove any food.

ENVIRONMENTAL HAZARDS

25. Toxic to birds.
26. Toxic to fish and birds.
27. Toxic to fish, birds and wildlife.
28. Toxic to fish and wildlife.
29. Highly toxic to bees exposed to direct treatment or residues on blooming crops or weeds.
30. Do not apply to humans, clothing or bedding.
31. Do not contaminate feed or food products.
32. Extremely toxic to fish.
33. Extremely toxic to fish and aquatic organisms.
34. May be hazardous to aquatic organisms.
35. Do not contaminate water or wetland, lakes, streams or ponds.
36. Do not contaminate feed or food products or food preparation surfaces, dishes, kitchen utensils and food containers.
37. Do not apply to humans, animals, clothing or bedding.
38. Do not use on or contaminate fruit, vegetables or other food or feed crops.
39. Cover or remove fish bowls and aquaria and birds.
40. Keep away from humans, domestic animals and pets.
41. If swallowed, this material may reduce the clotting ability of the blood and cause bleeding.
42. Birds and other wildlife in treated areas may be killed.
43. Birds feeding on the treated areas may be killed.
44. Do not apply when weather conditions favor drift from treated areas.
45. Keep away from food, feedstuffs and water supplies.
46. May kill or severely reduce plant growth.

Ask your pest control company to show you anywhere on the labels of the various "registered" pesticide poisons where it states: "This poison is safe for humans and/or pets."

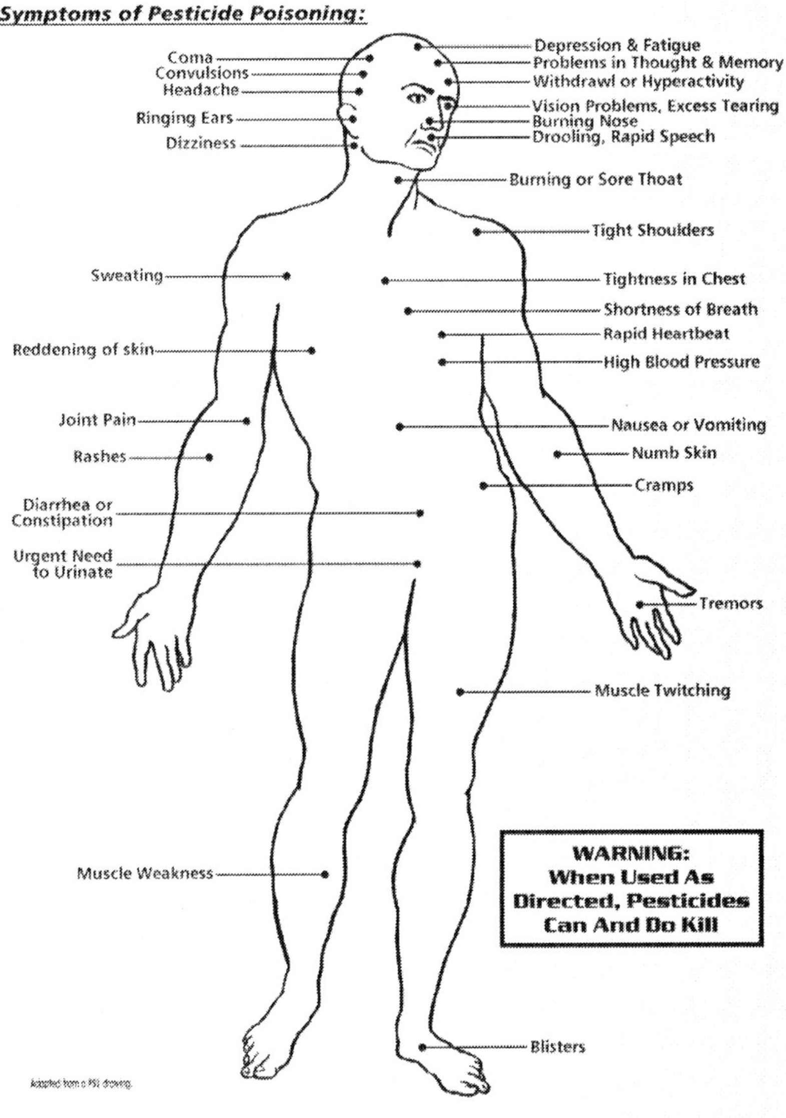
Symptoms of Pesticide Poisoning:
Coma
Convulsions
Headache
Ringing Ears
Dizziness
Depression & Fatigue
Problems in Thought & Memory
Withdrawl or Hyperactivity
Vision Problems, Excess Tearing
Burning Nose
Drooling, Rapid Speech
Burning or Sore Thoat
Tight Shoulders
Sweating
Tightness in Chest
Shortness of Breath
Rapid Heartbeat
Reddening of skin
High Blood Pressure
Joint Pain
Nausea or Vomiting
Rashes
Numb Skin
Cramps
Diarrhea or Constipation
Urgent Need to Urinate
Tremors
Muscle Twitching
WARNING: When Used As Directed, Pesticides Can And Do Kill
Muscle Weakness
Blisters

About the Author

Stephen L. Tvedten was President of Stroz Services, Inc. (an alternative pest control company) since 1970, until it *accidentally* burned to the ground 11/5/95 and is currently President of Get Set, Inc., an integrated pest management company and is also currently President of PEST (Prevent Environmental Suicide Today) an environmental group, and Steve is the founder of the Institute of Pest Management, Inc., Prescriptive Nutrients, Inc. and TIPM and the Natural Pest Control Association. Steve is Head of the Advisory Board for the Natural Pest Control Council of America. Steve was licensed as a Michigan Residential Builder and Maintenance Alteration Contractor and holds or has held Michigan pest control certifications in the following categories: Forest Pest Management, Wood Preservation, Turf, Ornamentals, Seed Treatment, Aquatic, swimming Pools, Cooling Towers, Right-of-way, Structural Pest Management, Wood Destroying Organisms, Vertebrate, Interiorscape, Mosquito and Public Health. Steve also holds or has held Texas pest control certifications in General, Pest Control and Termite control, New York certifications in termite, structural, pest and rodent control. Ohio pest control certification in the following categories: seed treatment, general aquatic, swimming pool, general forest pest, timber stand improvement, wood preservation, industrial vegetation control, ornamental plant and shade tree, interior plantscape, vertebrate animal control, turf pest control, domestic, institutional, structural and health related pest control, general pest, termite, mosquito, house fly and vector control and Wisconsin certifications in forest, ornamental and turf, seed treatment, aquatic, right-of-way, general industrial, institutional, structural and health related, termite and wood preservation; State of Illinois certifications in seed treatment, right-of-way, ornamental and turf, forest, aquatic and mosquito pest control; State of Indiana certifications for seed treatment, wood preservative non-pressured, forest, ornamental, aquatic, right-of-way, residential, institutional and non-food industry pest control. Steve has held West Virginia pest control certifications in general pest, structural pest, wood treatment and public health. Steve has been a science advisor for the National Pediculosis Association. Steve is a member of the Entomological Society of America. Steve is a member of The Xerces Society, the International Cockroach Society, Inc. and the International Organization for Biological Control of Noxious Animals and Plants, Neartic Regional Section. Steve is on the National Coalition for the Chemically Injured (NCCI) advisory board for proposed rules for IPM in schools. In addition Steve is or has been a certified home inspector, a certified termite inspector, a certified asbestos inspector and a certified environmental inspector. Steve developed the first guaranteed termite inspection program for real estate and the Get Set IPM program. Steve has written a monthly pest control column for *The Toxic Times* and is writing for the Journal of Alternative Medicine. Steve wrote "The Bug Stops Here, The Best Control and The Best Control II". Steve developed a computerized Phase I Environmental Inspection program and a complete computerized home inspection program. Steve has written several alternative pest control books and numerous pamphlets, articles and developed (self-help) Professionally Guided Pest Control programs to safely and permanently control roaches, fleas, all wood destroying organisms (decay fungi and insects), rodent and miscellaneous pests. Was the recipient of the 1985 Small Business of the Year Environmental Award. Has been on the guest faculty of environmental groups such as NCAMP and has written and testified before the U. S. House of Representatives on the Federal Insecticide, Fungicide and Rodenticide Act, the Environmental Protection Agency, the Michigan Toxic Substance Control Commission, the Michigan Department of Agriculture hearings and elsewhere regarding the safe use of chemicals. Steve has taken pest control courses from Purdue and Penn State Universities. Steve has taught a Post Graduate Course on PsychimmunNeuro Toxicology (Effects of Chemicals on Man) including treatment protocols at the Indiana Academy of Osteopathy. Steve is and has been consulted by lawyers, doctors, laboratories, environmentalists, government officials, victims, and reporters from all over this country and internationally. Steve has been a member of the National Writer's Union. Steve has numerous trademarks, copyrights and patents here in the USA and abroad.

"Imagination is more important than knowledge." -Einstein

"Men occasionally stumble over the truth, but most of them pick themselves up and hurry off as if nothing ever happened." -Winston Churchill

"Today's problems can not be solved by thinking the way we thought when we created them." -Einstein

"One of the most effective ways we can protect children is to provide adults with the information on how best to safeguard their families from environmental hazards." -Carol Browner, U. S. Environmental Protection Agency

Printed in the United States
33032LVS00008B/14

9 781418 440961